BASIC RADIO
vol. 3

REVISED SECOND EDITION

MARVIN TEPPER

HAYDEN BOOK COMPANY, INC.
Rochelle Park, New Jersey

ISBN 0-8104-5923-X
Library of Congress Catalog Card Number 73-6498

Hayden Book Company, Inc.
50 Essex Street, Rochelle Park, New Jersey 07662

Copyright © 1961, 1974

1 2 3 4 5 6 7 8 9   PRINTING

74 75 76 77 78   YEAR

PREFACE

Basic Radio is a course in communications electronics, as distinct from a general course in electronics. The text deals with the circuitry and techniques used for the transmission and reception of intelligence via radio energy. Assuming no prior knowledge of electricity or electronics, the six volumes of this course "begin at the beginning" and carry the reader in logical steps through the study of electricity and electronics required for a clear understanding of radio receivers and transmitters. Illustrations are used profusely to reinforce the highlights of the text. All examples given are based on actual or typical circuitry to make the course as practical and realistic as possible. Most important, the text provides a solid foundation upon which the reader can build his further, more advanced knowledge.

No prior knowledge of electricity or electronics is required for the understanding of this series. Because this series embraces a vast amount of information, it cannot be read like a novel, skimming through for the high points. Each topic contains a carefully selected thought or group of thoughts, so that each unit can be studied as a separate subject. Mathematics is kept to a minimum and, where necessary, the mathematical methods are fully explained.

This Revised Edition of *Basic Radio* retains the structure of the First Edition. Volume 1 treats d-c electricity. The slightly more involved subject of a-c electricity is presented in Volume 2. Equipped with this information, the reader is ready to study the operation of electron tubes and electron tube circuits in Volume 3, including power supplies, amplifiers, oscillators, etc. The components of electronic circuitry presented in Volumes 1 through 3 are assembled in Volume 4, which discusses the complete radio receiver, AM and FM. Volume 5 gives special attention to the theory and circuitry of transistors and integrated circuits. Volume 6 covers the long-neglected subject of transmitters, antennas, and transmission lines. In sum, the full range of the fundamentals of communications electronics is covered in a manner that provides maximum comprehension with a minimum of effort.

To the many people whose thoughts and discussions have contributed to this series, my sincere appreciation. To my wife, Celia, and my daughters, Ruth and Shirley, with whom I would have preferred to spend more time, my heartfelt thanks and gratitude for their assistance and understanding patience.

MARVIN TEPPER

Falmouth, Massachusetts

CONTENTS

vol. 3

BASIC RADIO
vol. 3

Development of the Electron Tube

In Volumes 1 and 2, we studied d-c and a-c electricity. In Volume 3, we learn about the electron tube and its associated circuitry, which takes us into the field of electronics. The electron tube has made possible the transmission and reception of music and speech over great distances, and its many applications have given birth to the communications industry. Although the electronics field has become quite vast, we shall be concerned primarily with radio electronics.

It can be said that the modern electron tube began with the phenomenon of the Edison Effect. Thomas A. Edison experimentally inserted a metal plate into the same glass bulb with a carbon wire filament, and connected it to the positive side of the battery used to heat the filament. Despite the open-circuit condition prevailing between the heated filament and the plate, Edison still measured some current flow on the galvanometer (sensitive ammeter) connected in series with the plate. He was unable to explain this situation, which came to be called the Edison Effect.

In 1899, Sir J. J. Thompson presented his electron theory as an explanation of the Edison Effect. Thompson said that electrons were emitted by the heated filament as a result of operating it at incandescence, or white heat. He said, further, that these electrons, because of their negative charge, were attracted to the positively charged plate. These electrons formed an electron current that bridged the filament-plate gap. Later development led to J. A. Fleming's "valve," a two-electrode, improved version of Edison's device. Finally, the three-electrode tube called the audion was invented by Lee De Forest in 1907; this gave the real impetus to the growth of the electronics industry by its ability to perform as an amplifier in many circuits.

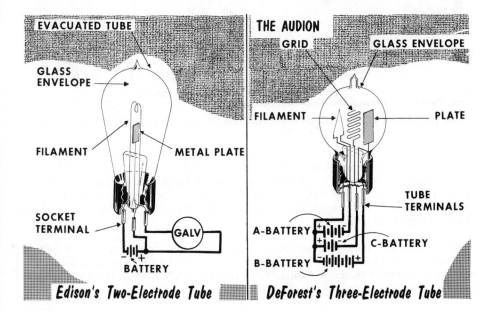

Edison's Two-Electrode Tube   *DeForest's Three-Electrode Tube*

Electron Tube Construction

Before discussing the operation of the various tube types, such as the diode, triode, tetrode, and pentode, we should become familiar with the basic construction of the electron tube. Because the vast majority of tubes used in radio communications are highly evacuated, we shall refer to them by their more popular name: vacuum tubes.

The most common material used in the construction of a vacuum tube envelope is glass. Many tube envelopes are made entirely of glass, and even in the so-called "metal" tubes, the electrode leads pass through a glass bead sealed into an eyelet. Some glass tubes, such as octal types, are fitted into a plastic base for convenience in handling. The electrodes in a vacuum tube are supported by insulators such as mica and a variety of ceramics. The electrodes themselves are commonly made from metals such as nickel, copper, aluminum, molybdenum, and tungsten.

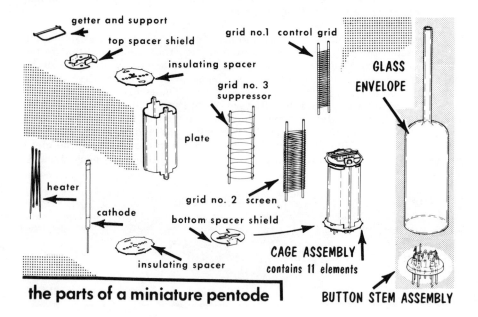

the parts of a miniature pentode

An important consideration is the creation of a high vacuum. Should there be a significant amount of air in the tube, the filament would burn up. To obtain the necessary vacuum, special vacuum pumps are used to bring the pressure in the vacuum tube down to less than 1/1,000,000,000 that of normal atmospheric pressure.

After a tube is evacuated and sealed, a magnesium or barium getter placed in the tube is used to remove residual gases by combining with them. The getter is flashed by an r-f induction process, which often leaves a visible silvery deposit on the wall of the tube.

Types of Electron Emission

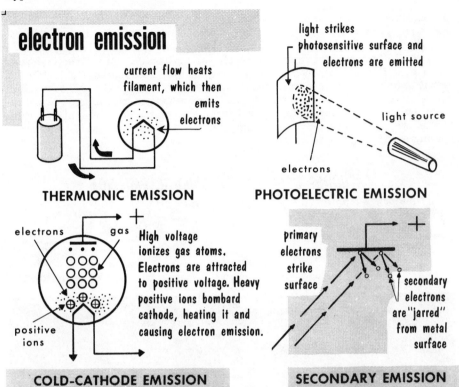

electron emission

THERMIONIC EMISSION

current flow heats filament, which then emits electrons

PHOTOELECTRIC EMISSION

light strikes photosensitive surface and electrons are emitted

light source

electrons

COLD-CATHODE EMISSION

electrons   gas

High voltage ionizes gas atoms. Electrons are attracted to positive voltage. Heavy positive ions bombard cathode, heating it and causing electron emission.

positive ions

SECONDARY EMISSION

primary electrons strike surface

secondary electrons are "jarred" from metal surface

In the discussion of the electron or vacuum tube, our starting point is logically the source of electrons — the filament or cathode. When the cathode is cold, these electrons roam freely within the cathode material, but generally do not fly off the metal into the surrounding air. The surface of the metal forms a "barrier" which prevents electrons from leaving. One way in which we can force electrons to break through the surface barrier is to increase their energy of motion. If the electron energy in the cathode material can be increased sufficiently, the electrons "boil off" the cathode surface in much the same way as water vaporizes at sufficient temperature. Of the several methods which exist for speeding up the movement of electrons, four are most frequently used. Most important is the heating of the cathode material which causes thermionic emission. The heating, which may be either direct or indirect, brings about electron emission. The electrons are liberated from the cathode surface which is covered with a special chemical coating such as alkaline-earth oxides. A second method (used with certain substances) is to project light onto the emitting surface to produce photoelectric emission. A third technique is to bombard the cathode with ions, producing cold-cathode emission, and the fourth, called secondary emission, is produced by fast-moving electrons striking a surface and releasing other electrons.

Thermionic Emission

In a vacuum tube, thermionic emission is obtained when the cathode is heated inside an evacuated envelope. This is accomplished by using the heating effect produced by an electric current passed through a conducting wire or heater. Cathodes may be heated directly or indirectly. In a directly heated cathode (called a filament, or filament-cathode), the heated element is the actual emitter of electrons. In an indirectly heated cathode (or heater-cathode), the heater is used only to heat the cathode to an emission temperature and does not contribute to the thermionic emission of the tube. Filaments are usually made of pure tungsten or thoriated tungsten, or have a coating of alkaline-earth oxide.

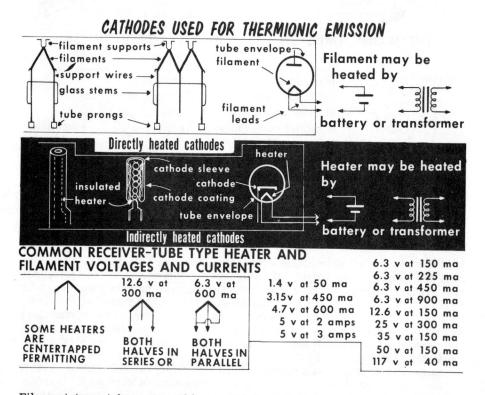

CATHODES USED FOR THERMIONIC EMISSION

Filament-type tubes are seldom used in radio receivers except in power supply applications; they do, however, find wide use in the higher-power tubes used in radio transmitters. Pure tungsten filaments are excellent emitters where high values of thermionic emission are desired, but they require extremely high operating temperatures of about 2500°C. Thoriated-tungsten filaments provide somewhat less emission, but operate at lower temperatures of about 1900°C. The most efficient electron emitters are the oxide-coated filaments and cathodes. Here, the emission takes place from the oxide coating, which provides excellent emission for low-power tubes at temperatures of about 1000°C.

The Diode

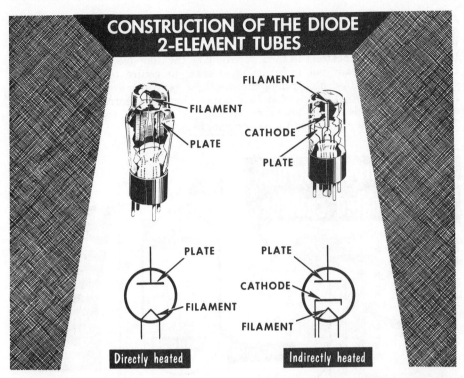

CONSTRUCTION OF THE DIODE
2-ELEMENT TUBES

FILAMENT

FILAMENT

PLATE

FILAMENT

CATHODE

PLATE

PLATE

FILAMENT

PLATE

CATHODE

FILAMENT

Directly heated

Indirectly heated

The simplest type of electron tube is the diode. It consists of two elements, or electrodes: one is the emitter of electrons and the other the collector of electrons. Both electrodes are enclosed in a glass or metal envelope which is then evacuated. Later, we shall study diodes that contain a certain amount of gas. In calling the diode a two-element tube, we consider the electron emitter as a single element, despite the fact that it might be a filament or a heater-cathode combination. The electron collector is the plate, and is sometimes referred to as the anode. We shall see that when the plate electrode is positive with respect to the cathode, it will attract electrons emitted from the cathode.

The primary function of the diode is rectification, about which we shall study later in this volume. In this function, the diode appears in two general constructions — signal diodes and power diodes. The signal types are generally small both in physical size and in their ability to handle currents and voltages. The power diode is usually relatively large, is built to handle high voltages and currents, and may become exceedingly hot during operation. Some diodes have a single cathode and plate, others have a single cathode and two plates, and still others have two cathodes and two plates. Where two plates are used in a single tube envelope, the tube is referred to as a duo-diode. The plate material must be able to withstand relatively high temperatures and usually is metal such as nickel, iron, or molybdenum.

Space Charge

Heating a filament or cathode in an evacuated envelope produces electron emission. But what happens to the emitted electrons? The first group of emitted electrons gathers in the space surrounding the cathode. The following group of electrons is then repelled by the like (negative) charges of the electrons already out in space, and start to return to the cathode. A third group of emitted electrons prevents their return by repelling them outward. The result of this action is a dense cloud of electrons in the space around the cathode, with fewer electrons further away from the cathode. This electron cloud is called the space charge.

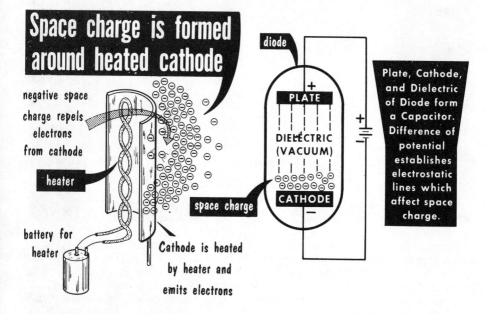

At first, it might seem that the electrons will continue to be emitted indefinitely. However, the negative space charge soon becomes so strong that it repels any additional emitted electrons back toward the cathode. This represents the maximum amount of electrons that could be emitted from the cathode unless the cathode temperature were raised. A temperature increase would cause more electrons to be released until a new equilibrium point were reached. As we shall see, the space charge is very useful in that it acts as a reservoir of electrons.

We have said that the diode is basically a two-element tube containing a cathode and a plate. From our study of capacitors, we see that these two elements, separated by an insulator (the vacuum in the tube), form a capacitor. If we place a difference of potential between cathode and plate, electrostatic lines will be established across the dielectric and will influence the space charge. If the plate is made positive with respect to the cathode, electrons from the negative space charge will be attracted to it.

Plate Current

Now that the electrons are in the form of a space charge, the problem is to put them to use. If another electrode is placed in the enclosed vacuum and given a positive charge with respect to the cathode, electrons will be attracted to it from the space charge. (The reduction of the space charge resulting from this permits more electrons to be emitted from the cathode.) A continuous positive voltage on the second electrode (called the anode or plate) can be maintained by connecting the positive terminal of a battery to it, while connecting the negative terminal to the cathode. This results in a continuous flow of electrons through the tube. These electrons then move to the positive terminal, through the battery, and finally complete the circuit by returning to the cathode.

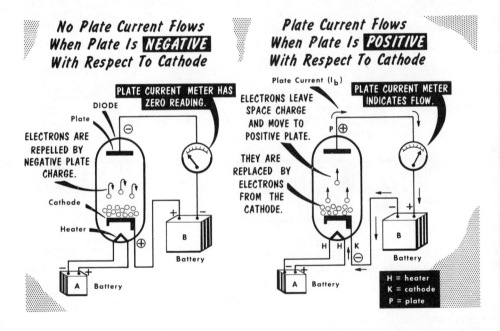

The electron flow through the vacuum is called the plate current (I_b). The voltage applied between plate and cathode is called the plate voltage (E_b), and the voltage source the B supply. (The voltage source used to heat the heater or filament is called the A supply.) We can control the flow of plate current in a diode two ways: by varying the cathode temperature; and by varying the difference of potential between plate and cathode (plate voltage). Cathodes are designed to operate most efficiently at one particular temperature, so variation of cathode temperature must be ruled out in favor of plate voltage variation. Control of plate current is relatively simple to maintain: increasing plate voltage increases plate current and decreasing plate voltage decreases plate current. If the negative terminal of the B supply is connected to the plate and the positive terminal to the cathode, the plate will repel all the emitted electrons, and there will be zero plate current.

Plate-Voltage, Plate-Current Curves

An important relationship in electron tubes exists between the voltage applied to the plate and the resultant plate current when the cathode temperature is held constant. If we place an ammeter in the plate circuit of the diode and slowly vary the voltage on the plate from zero to some high value (depending on the tube type), we notice a variation in plate current. As the plate voltage increases from zero to a slightly positive value, the amount of plate current (I_b) begins to increase gradually. As plate voltage (E_b) further increases, the plate current begins to increase at a fairly regular amount for a given change in plate voltage. Finally, a point is reached where increases in plate voltage produce less and less change in plate current. This point is called "saturation," and the plate is taking all the electrons available at the cathode for that given cathode temperature. At this saturation point, further increases in plate voltage produce virtually no change in plate current. Raising the cathode temperature produces more electron emission, but only at the expense of overworking the heater element.

If we were to make a graph by plotting the current value for all the plate voltage values, we would end up with a characteristic curve of the tube. This E_b-I_b curve provides, at a glance, the entire operating characteristic. Static curves generally show operation with no "load" or voltage variations in the tube circuit; dynamic curves generally show tube operation when there is a load and voltage variations in the tube circuit.

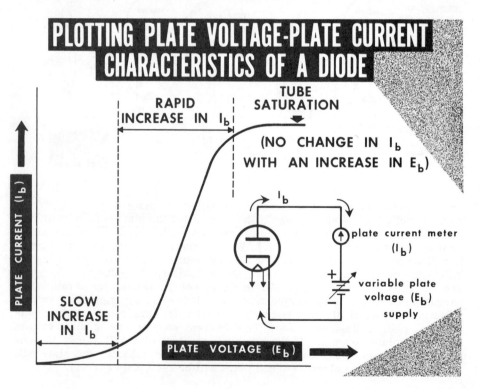

PLOTTING PLATE VOLTAGE-PLATE CURRENT CHARACTERISTICS OF A DIODE

RAPID INCREASE IN I_b

TUBE SATURATION

(NO CHANGE IN I_b WITH AN INCREASE IN E_b)

PLATE CURRENT (I_b)

I_b

plate current meter (I_b)

variable plate voltage (E_b) supply

SLOW INCREASE IN I_b

PLATE VOLTAGE (E_b)

Diode Plate Resistance – D-C

The d-c plate resistance of the diode is opposition to the flow of plate current offered by the tube when a d-c voltage is applied to the plate. From Ohm's law, we can develop the formula for d-c plate resistance, R_p. Using E_b and I_b for tube voltage and current, we get $R_p = E_b/I_b$. The d-c resistance of a diode depends upon many things, such as the size of the electrodes, temperature of the cathode, or distance between electrodes. We can calculate this resistance from the plate voltage-plate current characteristic of a tube. In the drawing, we see that when the plate voltage is 10 volts, 14 milliamperes (0.014 amp) of plate current flow. Since $R_p = 10/0.014$, the plate resistance at this point is 714.2 ohms. Going to 20 volts on the plate produces a plate current of 40 ma, and a diode plate resistance of 20/0.040, or 500 ohms. Taking one further reading at a plate voltage of 30 volts shows that the plate current has now risen to 74 ma, for a tube plate resistance of 30/0.074, or 405.4 ohms.

USING A TYPICAL DIODE STATIC CHARACTERISTIC TO OBTAIN THE D-C PLATE RESISTANCE

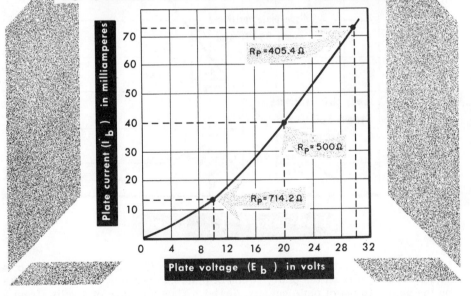

From these figures, we see that the resistance offered by the diode to the flow of plate current is not constant, as in a conventional resistor. The characteristic shows that the diode resistance decreases as the plate voltage increases, and increases as the plate voltage is decreased – it behaves non-linearly. If the I_b-E_b curve were a straight line, the resistance of the diode would be constant at all points on the curve.

Diode Plate Resistance – A-C

We can consider the a-c plate resistance of the diode as the resistance of the path between cathode and plate to the flow of an alternating current inside the tube.   We use the same curve for finding the diode a-c resistance as we did for the d-c resistance.   However, the a-c plate resistance (r_p) is the ratio of a small <u>change</u> in plate voltage to the small <u>change</u> in plate current that it produces.   Written in the style of Ohm's law, $r_p = \Delta e_p / \Delta i_p$. The Greek letter <u>delta</u> (Δ) means "a small change in. " Thus, to find the a-c resistance of a diode, we consider <u>changes</u> in plate voltage and <u>changes</u> they produce in plate current.

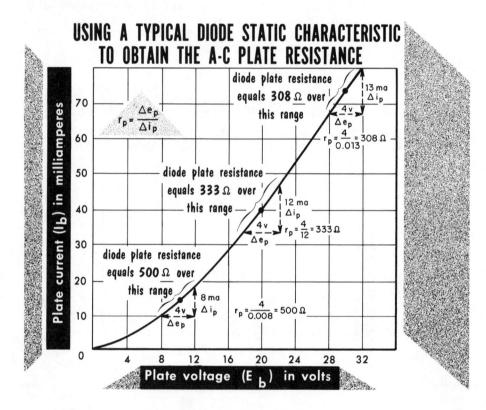

USING A TYPICAL DIODE STATIC CHARACTERISTIC TO OBTAIN THE A-C PLATE RESISTANCE

If we change the plate voltage from 8 volts to 12 volts, there is a change of 4 volts. With 8 volts on the plate, 10 ma of plate current flowed. With 12 volts on the plate, 18 ma of plate current flowed. Thus a change of 4 volts (from 8 to 12) on the plate produced a change of 8 ma (from 10 to 18) of plate current. The a-c plate resistance over this portion of the curve is then: $r_p = 4/0.008$, or 500 ohms. Using the same points on the curve as in d-c plate resistance and varying the plate voltage 2 volts above and below these points, we get a-c plate resistances of 333 ohms and 307 ohms over these ranges. From this, we can see that when the plate resistance of a tube is mentioned, it is always with respect to a particular point on the tube's characteristic curve.

Static and Dynamic Diode Characteristics

So far, we have discussed static conditions in the diode, where no load was in the circuit. Much more important are the dynamic conditions of the diode circuit. For a diode, or any tube, to perform its normal function, its external circuit must contain a load. It is through this load that the diode current flows outside the tube, and the voltage drop developed across this load then represents the output of the tube. The load resistance is given the symbol R_L.

With no load resistance in the circuit, virtually all circuit resistance consists of the diode plate resistance. However, when an external load resistance is added, the total opposition to plate current flow includes the tube plate resistance plus the load resistance. When the load resistance is many times greater than the plate resistance, it is primarily R_L that determines the shape of the characteristic curve. Note that the larger the load resistance, the less the curvature in the characteristic. As we shall learn later, a linear or straight dynamic characteristic is important because it provides proportionality between changes in plate voltage and the accompanying changes in plate current. This in turn provides freedom from distortion — important in many diode circuits.

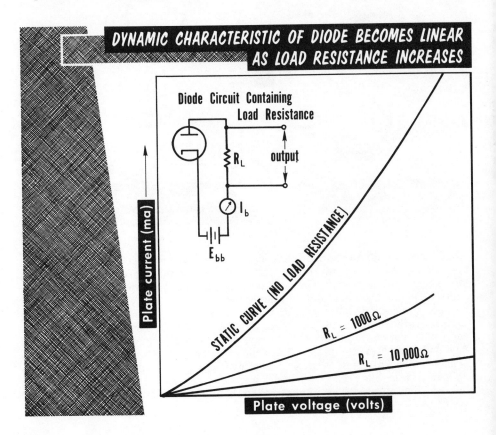

DYNAMIC CHARACTERISTIC OF DIODE BECOMES LINEAR AS LOAD RESISTANCE INCREASES

The Triode

The invention of the triode was an extremely important advance in electronics because it permitted electronic "amplification." Basically, the triode is nothing more than a diode to which has been added a third electrode – a grid. Physically, the grid is a ladder-like structure of metal. In most instances, it has a helical form and consists of a number of turns of fine wire wound in the grooves of two upright metal supports. The physical dimensions of the grid determine many of the operating characteristics of the triode.

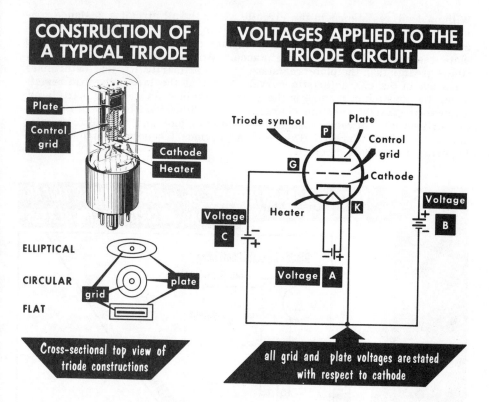

CONSTRUCTION OF A TYPICAL TRIODE

Plate
Control grid
Cathode
Heater

ELLIPTICAL
CIRCULAR
FLAT

plate
grid

Cross-sectional top view of triode constructions

VOLTAGES APPLIED TO THE TRIODE CIRCUIT

Triode symbol
Plate
P
Control grid
G
Cathode
K
Voltage B
Voltage C
Heater
Voltage A

all grid and plate voltages are stated with respect to cathode

The basic function of the grid is to control the movement of electrons between the cathode and plate, thereby controlling the amount of plate current flowing in the tube. It is for this reason that this third electrode is given the name control grid. The control grid may be wound around the cathode in the space between the cathode and plate, or merely exist as a screen-like mesh between parallel cathode and plate surfaces. Because it is so very close to the cathode, voltages on the control grid exert much more influence on plate current than do voltages on the plate. Since the cathode is generally taken as the reference point, all plate and grid voltages are measured with respect to the cathode. D-c plate voltages are known as "B" voltages, d-c grid voltages (called "bias") as "C" voltages, and heater, or filament voltages as "A" voltages.

Electrostatic Field in Triode

The control grid in the triode serves primarily as an electrostatic shield between the plate and cathode, and allows some, but not all, of the electrostatic field from the plate to get to the cathode. When the grid is at the same
potential as the cathode, it exerts no electrostatic influence, and the triode
acts just as a diode. However, when the control grid is made negative with
respect to the cathode, it sets up an electrostatic field in opposition to the
cathode-plate field. The action of a negative grid is to repel electrons from
the cathode back to the cathode. At the same time, the positive plate acts to
attract electrons from the cathode to the plate. The net effect is a compromise, depending upon the relative grid and plate voltages. Since the grid is
so close to the cathode, a relatively small grid voltage has as much influence
as a much larger plate voltage.

When the grid is made slightly negative, some electrons from the cathode
are repelled back, but many others pass through the wire mesh grid structure and are attracted to the positive plate. It is possible that, for a given
plate voltage, the grid voltage can be made sufficiently negative to cut off the
flow of plate current completely. On the other hand, the grid (bias) voltage
could be made so positive as to produce plate current saturation, with further
increases in grid voltage having no effect on plate current. When the grid is
positive with respect to cathode, some electrons are attracted to the grid
structure and produce a flow of grid current. The control grid is most
commonly operated at a voltage slightly negative with respect to the cathode.

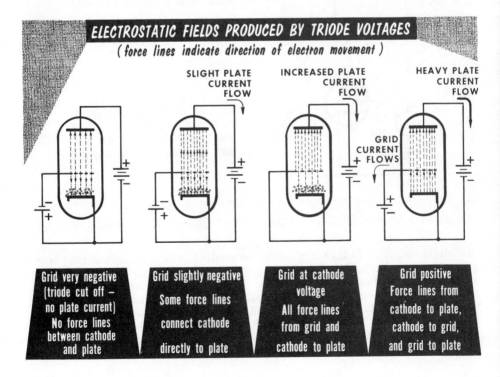

ELECTROSTATIC FIELDS PRODUCED BY TRIODE VOLTAGES
(force lines indicate direction of electron movement)

SLIGHT PLATE CURRENT FLOW INCREASED PLATE CURRENT FLOW HEAVY PLATE CURRENT FLOW

GRID CURRENT FLOWS

Grid very negative
(triode cut off —
no plate current)
No force lines
between cathode
and plate

Grid slightly negative
Some force lines
connect cathode
directly to plate

Grid at cathode
voltage
All force lines
from grid and
cathode to plate

Grid positive
Force lines from
cathode to plate,
cathode to grid,
and grid to plate

Steady-State Condition of a Triode Circuit

The basic triode circuit consists of the grid-cathode portion called the input and the plate-cathode portion called the output. In this circuit, all input voltages or signals are applied between grid and cathode; all output voltages or signals appear between plate and cathode. Thus, we see that the cathode is the element common to both input and output circuits. The voltage applied to the plate or anode of the tube is positive with respect to the cathode and, in typical circuits, may vary from 100 to 300 volts. In most receiver circuits, the control grid is kept at a voltage slightly negative with respect to the cathode. Hence, it acts to limit or control the amount of electron flow between cathode and plate.

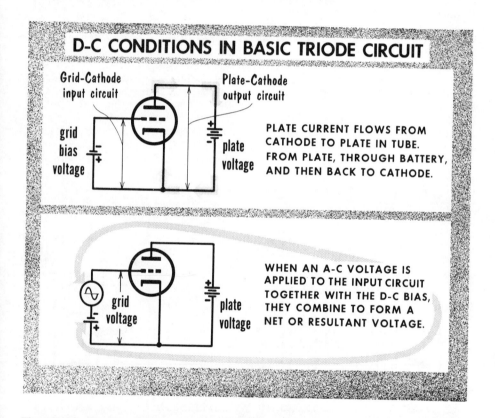

D-C CONDITIONS IN BASIC TRIODE CIRCUIT

Grid-Cathode input circuit   Plate-Cathode output circuit

grid bias voltage   plate voltage

PLATE CURRENT FLOWS FROM CATHODE TO PLATE IN TUBE. FROM PLATE, THROUGH BATTERY, AND THEN BACK TO CATHODE.

grid voltage   plate voltage

WHEN AN A-C VOLTAGE IS APPLIED TO THE INPUT CIRCUIT TOGETHER WITH THE D-C BIAS, THEY COMBINE TO FORM A NET OR RESULTANT VOLTAGE.

The slight negative voltage applied to the control grid is called the bias voltage. For the moment, we shall assume that the plate and bias voltages are obtained through the use of batteries. With no input voltage applied to the circuit, a small steady plate current will flow. The amount will depend upon the values of positive plate voltage and negative grid voltage. This is often referred to as the steady-state condition of the circuit — when no external voltage is applied to the input circuit. These conditions change when an a-c voltage (signal) is applied to the input circuit.

Effect of Grid Voltage on Plate Current

Let us now apply an a-c voltage to the input circuit in addition to the fixed grid bias voltage. We shall assume that the a-c voltage has a peak of 5 volts, and that the steady-state d-c grid bias is -6 volts. At 0°, or the beginning of the input cycle, the 6-volt negative bias permits a plate current flow of 20 milliamperes (ma). At 90° of the input cycle, the a-c component of the grid voltage has risen to its maximum positive value, +5 volts. This voltage, added to the steady -6 volts, produces a net grid voltage of -1 volt with respect to the cathode. The grid voltage is still negative, but now it is only slightly negative, and plate current increases to its maximum of 30 ma.

From 90° to 180°, the input signal returns to zero, which added to the 6-volt negative bias produces a grid bias of -6 volts. The plate current thus drops back to its steady-state value of 20 ma. From 180° to 270°, the input voltage increases to its maximum negative value, -5 volts, which is added to the fixed bias, producing a total grid voltage of -11 volts. This large negative grid voltage reduces the plate current to 10 ma. From here, the plate current rises back to its steady value of 20 ma as the input voltage also rises back to its 360° value of zero volts. From this, we see that the plate current waveform follows the grid voltage, increasing as the grid is made less negative and decreasing as the grid becomes more negative.

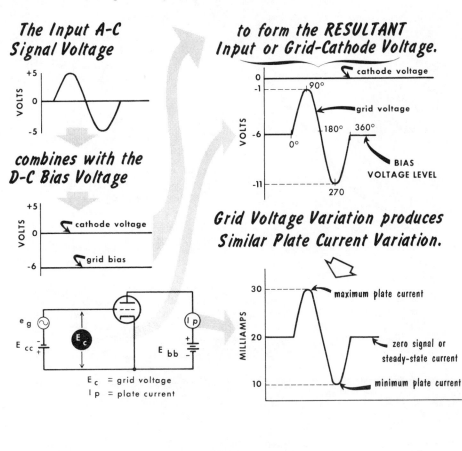

The Input A-C Signal Voltage

to form the RESULTANT Input or Grid-Cathode Voltage.

combines with the D-C Bias Voltage

Grid Voltage Variation produces Similar Plate Current Variation.

E c = grid voltage
I p = plate current

Triode Plate-Current, Grid-Voltage Curve

The relationships among the various voltages applied to the triode and the effects they have on the plate current are very important. As in the case of the diode, these relationships are shown through the use of characteristic curves. Basically, plate current in a triode is determined by the grid and plate voltages, assuming that the cathode remains at a constant temperature. We shall consider the grid voltage first, and assume that the plate voltage remains constant. We can then construct a plate-current, grid-voltage (I_b-E_g) curve by varying the grid voltage first in a positive direction from zero, and then in a negative direction. The plate current at various grid voltages is then plotted. This curve is called the static plate-current, grid-voltage characteristic, because it represents the tube behavior under no-load conditions. The plate and grid voltage are simply those of their respective supply voltages, and there are no voltage drops across load resistors.

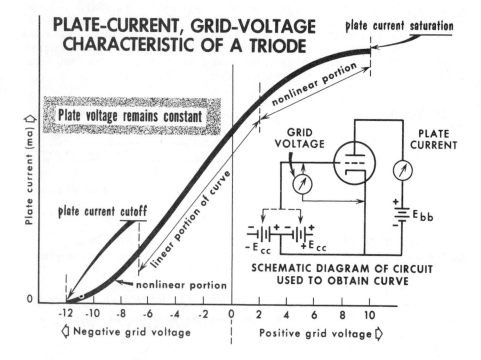

Note that the curve shown drops to zero at -12 volts. This point is known as cutoff and represents the minimum negative grid voltage needed to reduce plate current to zero. As the grid is made less negative, plate current begins to flow. The rise is gradual at first, then more rapid over the linear portion of the curve. Finally, the curve reaches a point where further increases in positive grid voltage produce no further increases in plate current. This is known as plate current saturation. We will see that most amplifiers operate on the linear portion of the curve between the cutoff and saturation areas.

Family of Grid Characteristic Curves

A single plate-current, grid-voltage characteristic curve furnishes important information, but is of limited value. A number of such curves shown on the same scale for different values of plate voltage give much more information concerning the effects of various grid voltages on plate current. Such curves, plotted on a single graph, comprise a "family" of characteristic curves. As a rule, the grid family of characteristic curves does not involve the positive region of grid voltage because, for most triode applications, the grid is not driven positive with respect to the cathode. The family of curves shown are for a typical triode. These curves are made as just described, except that the plate voltage was changed for every series of grid voltage variations. Note the close similarity among the general shapes of the characteristic curves: each curve has a linear portion and a nonlinear portion.

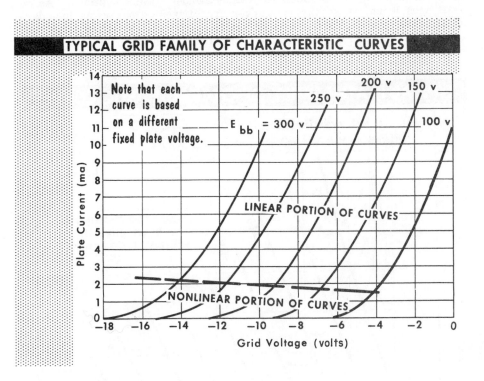

From this family of grid curves, we can see that the higher the positive plate voltage, the higher the negative grid voltage required to cut the tube off (reduce plate current to zero). In addition, the higher the plate voltage, the more plate current will flow for any given grid voltage. For purposes of amplification, we should remember that proportional changes (ratio of plate current to grid voltage) occur only over the linear (straight) parts of the curve. The greatest change in plate current per unit change in grid voltage occurs along the straight (rather than the curved) portion of the characteristic.

Triode Plate-Current, Plate-Voltage Curves

As in the case of the grid family of **curves**, we can make use of a plate family of curves. For every curve in this group, a particular grid voltage is held constant while the plate voltage is varied. In every instance, the plate current range shown for a particular fixed grid voltage starts at the point along the plate voltage axis where the negative grid voltage causes approximate plate current cutoff. In general, the grid family and plate family of curves furnish the same information; however, in somewhat different forms.

Where the grid family displays the plate current for small changes or increments of grid voltage and fixed differences in plate voltage, the plate family displays the plate current for small increments of plate voltage and fixed differences of grid voltage. These family graphs present the relationship between the different triode electrode voltages under static conditions. As we shall soon learn, these various curves are of tremendous value in understanding the operation of tubes under varied conditions. Virtually every tube type has its own set of grid and plate characteristics which are often shown in tube manuals and technical data sheets issued by tube manufacturers.

TYPICAL PLATE FAMILY OF CHARACTERISTIC CURVES

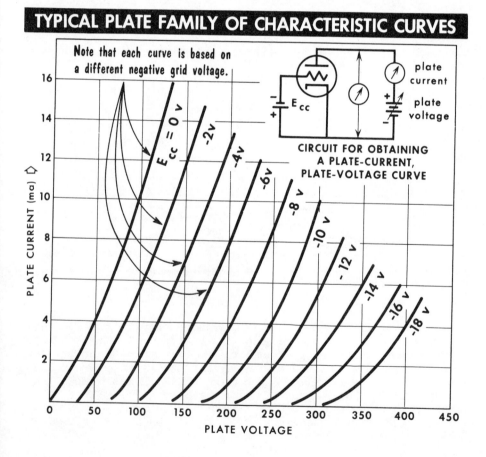

Note that each curve is based on a different negative grid voltage.

CIRCUIT FOR OBTAINING
A PLATE-CURRENT,
PLATE-VOLTAGE CURVE

Amplification Factor

Vacuum tubes have special figures of merit called tube constants. As we shall learn, these constants are used for tetrodes and pentodes, as well as for triodes. The three most commonly used tube constants are the amplification factor, symbolized by the Greek letter μ, plate resistance r_p, and mutual conductance g_m. Understanding their meaning and significance permits us to look at tube specifications and determine important design and operating characteristics of electron tubes.

Amplification factor tells us of the relative influence of grid voltage as compared to plate voltage on the amount of plate current flow in an electron tube. We could say that the amplification factor of a triode is equal to the ratio of a change (Δ) in plate voltage to a change in grid voltage in the opposite direction, under the condition that the plate current remain constant. Another way of stating it is to say that μ is equal to the ratio of a change in plate voltage to a change in grid voltage that results in the same change in plate current. As a formula, we say:

$$\mu = \frac{\Delta e_p}{\Delta e_g}$$

or a change in plate voltage divided by change in grid voltage (plate current remaining constant). For example, suppose that a 1-ma plate current change could be produced by a change in grid voltage of 0.1 volt, and a 1-ma plate current change was produced by a change in plate voltage of 10 volts. Such a tube would have an amplification factor of 10/0.1, or 100. This is a relatively high μ, and such a tube is called a high-μ tube. Low-μ tubes have an amplification factor of 10 or so. Between 10 and 30, we have the medium-μ tubes; above 30, a tube is considered to have a high μ. As can be seen, the μ of a tube can vary slightly, depending upon which portion of the curve is used.

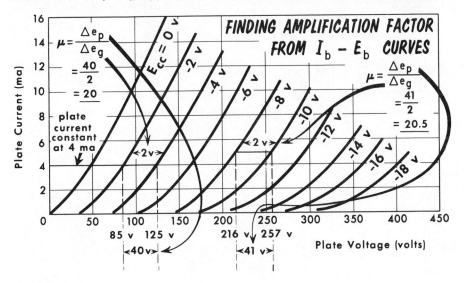

Plate Resistance

The plate resistance of a tube describes its internal resistance — that is, the opposition to electron flow between cathode and plate inside the tube. The d-c plate resistance expresses the steady-state resistance. This occurs when fixed voltages are on the control grid and plate. Under such conditions, the d-c plate resistance (R_p) can be determined by Ohm's law. We can thus say:

$$R_p = \frac{E_{(d\text{-}c \text{ plate voltage})}}{I_{(d\text{-}c \text{ plate current})}}$$

We can find R_p by taking any point on any of the plate family of curves, and then projecting down to the plate voltage and across to the plate current axes. We then solve by $R_p = E_b/I_b$.

Finding a-c plate resistance (r_p) is somewhat more involved, because this involves changes in plate voltage and plate current. We start by taking any point on any of the plate family of curves. We project a line horizontally from the curve — this represents a change in plate voltage. We then project a line upward vertically back to the curve — this line represents a change in plate current. By using the a-c equivalent of Ohm's law for plate resistance ($r_p = \Delta e_p/\Delta i_p$), we get the answer. Note that R_p concerns itself with a particular operating point, whereas r_p represents an operating range. Note also that the higher the applied plate voltage for a particular grid voltage, the lower is the a-c plate resistance. This is because the curves become steeper as they advance toward the higher plate voltages. This means that for a particular increase in plate voltage, there will be a disproportionately greater increase in plate current. The importance of r_p will be seen in our study of amplifiers.

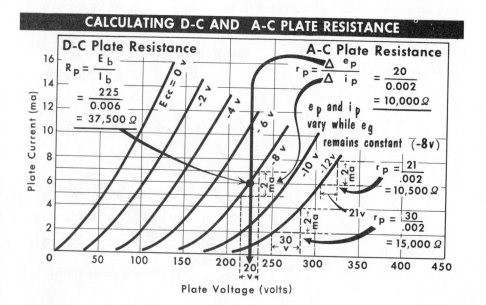

Transconductance (Mutual Conductance)

The third important tube constant discussed here is transconductance, also referred to as mutual conductance. By definition, transconductance is the quotient of a small change in plate current divided by the small change in the control grid voltage producing it, under the condition that all other tube voltages remain the same (in a triode this would refer to the plate and heater voltages). As an equation, transconductance, $g_m = \Delta i_p / \Delta e_g$. Transconductance is a measurement of conductance rather than resistance. As such, it is measured in mhos, mho being the reversed spelling of ohm. In practical tube circuitry, the mho is a rather large unit of measurement. To make it more workable, we use the micromho (μmho), one-millionth of a mho.

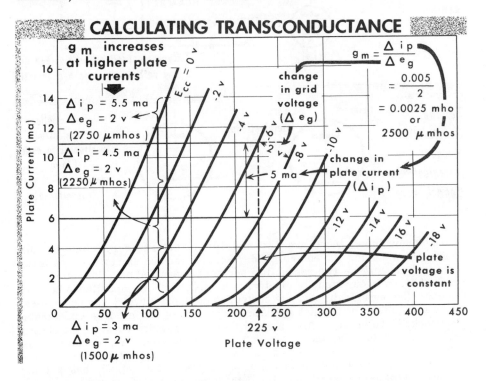

CALCULATING TRANSCONDUCTANCE

If a change of 1 volt on the control grid produces a change of 1 ma in plate current, our formula for transconductance ($g_m = 0.001/1$) would show that such a tube had a g_m of 0.001 mho, or 1000 μmhos. Transconductance is an excellent measure of how "good" a tube is. A tube having a high transconductance is capable of furnishing greater signal output than a tube with a low g_m, assuming that the same circuitry and voltages are applied to both tubes. The transconductance of most vacuum tubes varies from about 2000 to 9000 μmhos. To calculate g_m from the plate family of curves, we project along a constant-voltage line from one grid voltage curve to another. The difference in grid voltage divided by the difference in plate current, projected across to the plate current axis, gives us the g_m over this operating range.

The Tetrode

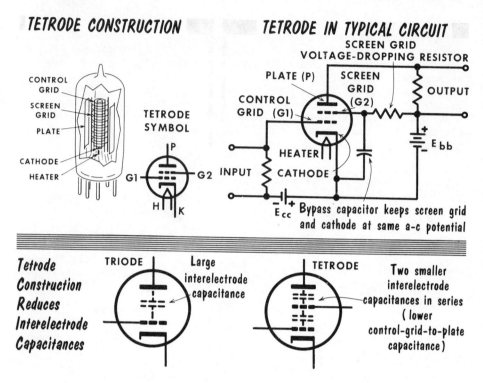

TETRODE CONSTRUCTION

CONTROL GRID
SCREEN GRID
PLATE
CATHODE
HEATER

TETRODE SYMBOL

TETRODE IN TYPICAL CIRCUIT

SCREEN GRID
VOLTAGE-DROPPING RESISTOR

PLATE (P)   SCREEN GRID (G2)
CONTROL GRID (G1)
HEATER
CATHODE
INPUT
OUTPUT
E_{bb}
E_{cc} Bypass capacitor keeps screen grid and cathode at same a-c potential

Tetrode Construction Reduces Interelectrode Capacitances

TRIODE — Large interelectrode capacitance

TETRODE — Two smaller interelectrode capacitances in series (lower control-grid-to-plate capacitance)

In the triode tube, there are two metallic structures very close to each other — the plate and the control grid. Since a vacuum exists between them, we have a capacitor — two conducting surfaces separated by a dielectric. As we shall learn in our study of electron tube circuitry, the capacitance between the plate (output circuit) and the control grid (input circuit) can become extremely troublesome at high operating frequencies and produce undesirable "feedback." To prevent this, a second grid is inserted between the control grid and the plate to act as a "screen" between the two. Appropriately, this second grid is called the screen grid. An electron tube containing both a control grid and a screen grid is called a tetrode. The tetrode has a finely wound control grid surrounding the cathode or emitter of electrons which, in turn, is surrounded by a coarser screen grid at a considerably greater distance out from the cathode. The screen grid, then, is surrounded by the plate.

To serve as an effective electrostatic shield, the screen grid is usually at a signal or a-c potential equal to that of the cathode, so that no voltage exists between these two electrodes. This is not to be confused with the d-c potential on the screen grid, which is very often approximately the same as the positive plate voltage. To obtain a "zero" a-c potential on the screen grid, a capacitor is connected between the screen grid and "ground" or cathode to act as a short circuit to the signal voltages.

Tetrode Characteristics

When the proper voltages are applied to the tetrode, electrons are attracted from the cathode to the plate. The screen grid, being positive with respect to the cathode, also attracts electrons. However, because of the comparatively large space between the screen grid wires, most of the electrons attracted by the screen grid pass through it to the plate. Thus the screen grid produces a strong electrostatic force that attracts electrons from the cathode, leaving the plate with very little electrostatic force on electrons emitted from the cathode. This results in an important effect: as long as the plate voltage is higher than the screen voltage, the plate current depends primarily on the screen grid voltage. As we shall learn, because the plate current in this tube is largely independent of plate voltage, it is possible to obtain much higher amplification with a tetrode than with a triode.

From the plate family of characteristic curves, we note that after an initial early rise, plate current decreases until the plate voltage is equal to the screen grid voltage. Following this, plate current increases sharply, and finally levels off slightly, having a small linear increase with plate voltage.

"Secondary emission" effects are brought about when electrons are dislodged from the plate by bombardment from regular cathode emission. Dislodged electrons are then attracted to the screen grid, resulting in a loss of plate current. These effects produce the decrease in plate current at low plate voltages and, in effect, give the tetrode a negative resistance over this range. The amplification factor and plate resistance of a tetrode are considerably higher than that of a triode; transconductance is not too high. Tetrodes are seldom used in radio receivers; they do find use, however, in transmitters.

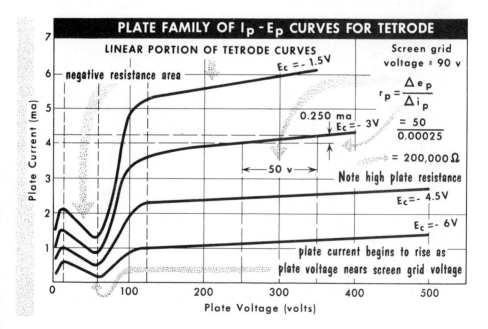

PLATE FAMILY OF I_p-E_p CURVES FOR TETRODE

LINEAR PORTION OF TETRODE CURVES

negative resistance area

$E_c = -1.5V$

Screen grid voltage = 90 v

$$r_p = \frac{\Delta e_p}{\Delta i_p}$$

0.250 ma

$E_c = -3V$

$$= \frac{50}{0.00025}$$

$$= 200,000\,\Omega$$

←—50 v—→

Note high plate resistance

$E_c = -4.5V$

$E_c = -6V$

plate current begins to rise as plate voltage nears screen grid voltage

Plate Current (ma)

Plate Voltage (volts)

The Pentode

The pentode is a five-element electron tube containing a cathode, a plate, a control grid, a screen grid, and a suppressor grid. The suppressor eliminates or suppresses secondary emission of electrons from the plate, thus removing the major drawback of the tetrodes. In addition, the capacitance between the control grid and plate now consists of three capacitances in series: there is capacitance between control grid and screen grid, screen grid and suppressor grid, and suppressor grid and plate. This reduces the value of the plate-to-control-grid capacitance still further, enabling the pentode to operate at still higher frequencies.

The suppressor grid is a coarse wire mesh placed between the screen grid and plate. It is usually connected to the cathode, which places it at a negative potential with respect to plate and screen grid. Because it is placed beyond the screen grid, its action does not interfere with that of the screen grid in attracting electrons. Moreover, because its wires are relatively widely spaced, it does not interfere with the fast-moving electrons which travel to the plate. When electrons striking the plate cause secondary emission, the negative potential of the suppressor grid repels them back to the positively charged plate, suppressing the secondary emission. Note that for a typical pentode, when the plate voltage is below 100 volts, there is no dip in the curve, which merely shows an increase in plate current with an increase in plate voltage. Above approximately 50 volts on the plate, the curves are relatively flat. This indicates that changes in plate voltage above this value have very little effect on plate current flow. Since the plate current is relatively independent of plate voltage, the two important factors to consider are screen grid voltage and control grid voltage. Screen grid voltage is fixed; hence, the control grid emerges as the major factor in controlling plate current flow. The amplification factor of pentodes may exceed 400, and the plate resistance is often in excess of 1 megohm. Transconductance of pentodes compares favorably with that of triodes and tetrodes, often being in the area of 5000 μmhos.

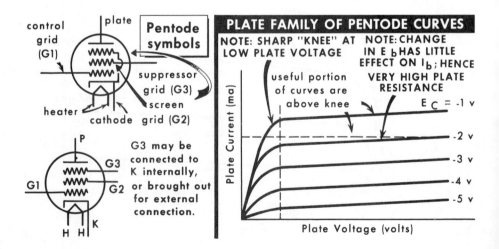

Beam Power Tubes

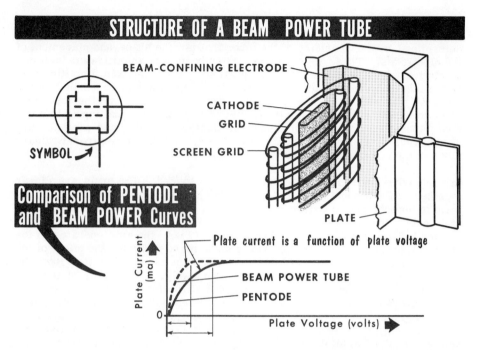

STRUCTURE OF A BEAM POWER TUBE

BEAM-CONFINING ELECTRODE

CATHODE

GRID

SYMBOL

SCREEN GRID

PLATE

Comparison of PENTODE and BEAM POWER Curves

Plate current is a function of plate voltage

Plate Current (ma)

BEAM POWER TUBE

PENTODE

0

Plate Voltage (volts)

In many ways, the beam power tube is a cross between a tetrode and a pentode. It is capable of handling high power levels, an ability obtained from that part of its design which concentrates the plate current electrons into sheets or beams of moving charges. In the beam power tube, the screen and control grids are wound in helical form so that each turn of the screen grid is shaded from the cathode by a turn of the control grid. It is this construction which causes electrons emitted from the cathode to be formed into beams, and reduces the amount of wasteful screen current flow. The beam-forming plates, used to confine the electron beam, are connected internally. Because the screen grid and plate are operated at approximately the same d-c potential, an effect equivalent to a space charge is developed in the space between the screen and plate. This effect is often called a "virtual cathode," and repels secondary electrons dislodged from the plate back to the plate, allowing high plate current efficiency. In some beam power tubes, the beam-forming plates are replaced with a conventional suppressor grid.

Note that the plate current of the beam power tube rises much more rapidly than that of the pentode. This shows that the region in which the plate current is primarily a function of the plate voltage is much smaller in the beam tube; that is, the plate current becomes independent of plate voltage at much lower values of plate voltage. This characteristic enables the beam power tube to handle much more power at lower values of plate voltage than an ordinary pentode. The beam power tube is extremely popular for the power output stages of radio receivers.

Variable-Mu Tubes

The amplification factor of a tube has been described as being equal to Δe_p Δe_g, with i_p remaining constant. This characteristic of a tube is largely determined by the geometry of the tube; that is, the shape and placement of the electrodes. Thus, we have gone on the basis that amplification factor is a relatively fixed characteristic of a particular tube. A fixed amplification-factor tube represents a problem when large signals are to be handled, since the grid bias voltage is driven highly negative at times, and the tube goes close to or into cutoff. To minimize distortion in large signal inputs to electron tubes, special kinds of high-amplification tetrodes and pentodes are used. These are known as variable-mu tubes, and they differ from ordinary tubes in the construction of their control grids.

In these tubes, the grid wires are unequally spaced. The turns are closer together at the top and bottom of the winding, and wider at the center. This form of control grid construction produces a tube which does not have a constant gain. Instead, its amplification changes with the value of grid voltage applied to the control grid. At low values of bias, the grid operates in the normal manner. As the control grid is made more negative, the effect of the closely spaced grid wires becomes greater, and the electron flow from the space charge in this region is cut off completely. The center of the grid structure also displays a greater effect, but still allows electrons to advance to the screen grid and plate. The overall reduction in plate current, therefore, is gradual. Eventually, with sufficient negative voltage on the grid, all parts of the grid winding act to cut off the plate current, but the negative grid voltage required to attain this is perhaps three to four times as much as for the conventional tube operated at similar screen and plate voltages. Thus, variable-mu tubes are used where it is desired to control transconductance by varying the control grid potential of the tube.

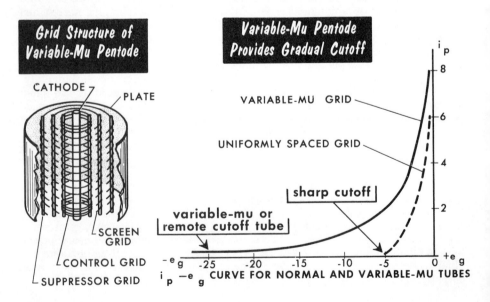

Grid Structure of Variable-Mu Pentode

CATHODE
PLATE
SCREEN GRID
CONTROL GRID
SUPPRESSOR GRID

Variable-Mu Pentode Provides Gradual Cutoff

i_p

VARIABLE-MU GRID

UNIFORMLY SPACED GRID

8
6
4
2

| sharp cutoff |

variable-mu or
| remote cutoff tube |

$-e_g$ -25   -20   -15   -10   -5   0 $+e_g$
i_p $-e_g$ CURVE FOR NORMAL AND VARIABLE-MU TUBES

Multigrid and Multi-unit Tubes

typical multi-unit tube arrangements

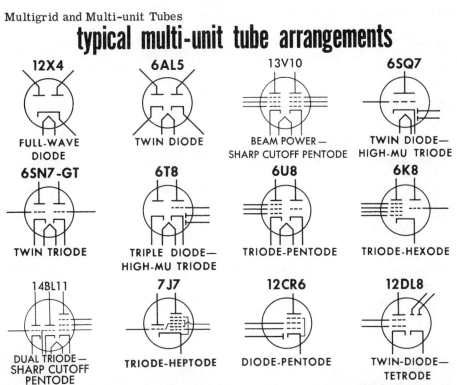

Our discussion of tubes so far has been related to "conventional" types such as the diode, triode, tetrode, and pentode. These tube constructions serve virtually all needs in electron tube receiver circuitry. However, one more must be considered for completeness – the heptode (7-elements), or pentagrid tube. This tube contains a plate, five grids, and a cathode (as in the 6BY6), or a directly heated filament (as in the 1R5). A tube of this type will very often have more than one signal input applied to it. (The same is true of the six-grid 7A8.)

Recent years have seen the combining of tube units or sections in one tube envelope. This permits circuit economy and compactness, since two or more circuits operate from one tube type. In some instances, the tube units are completely independent, having separate cathodes. In other instances, two tube units may operate from a single (common) cathode. Perhaps the simplest multi-unit tube is the twin diode 6AL5, containing merely two separate diodes. An example of complexity in multi-unit tubes is the 6K8 triode-hexode, which contains a triode and hexode (four grids) in one envelope. When more then one grid is used in a tube, they are usually numbered G1, G2, G3, etc., beginning with the grid closest to the cathode. In addition, tubes are often described by a characteristic or function (low-mu triode, pentagrid converter, etc.). Special dual and triple tubes have been developed for use in FM and television receivers. Examples of these are the 13V10 (a sharp cutoff pentode and beam power amplifier) and the 14BL11 (a dual triode and sharp cutoff pentode).

Vacuum Tube Designation and Basing

Vacuum tubes have undergone several changes in standardizing their type
styles. In the early days of radio, tube types such as VT1 and 201A were
used. This was followed by a numbering system, such as types 40 or 43.
Since the mid-thirties, however, a more formalized system has been developed in which the first number of a tube type indicates the heater or filament voltage. The letters and numbers that follow give an indication of the
tube's function and number of useful elements. However, in recent years,
the heavy flow of new tube types made much of this designation inexact. For
instance, the 35C5 requires a heater voltage of 35 volts; the 6BZ7 requires a
heater voltage of 6.3 volts; the 1U4 requires 1.4 volts for its heater; and the
117Z6-GT requires a heater voltage of 117 volts. In all instances, a tube
manual should be referred to in order to determine the exact heater voltage
and current requirements. Some tube types may use suffixes such as -G,
-GT, -GTA, and -GTB to indicate later modifications in the tube structure,
but the tube characteristics remain essentially the same.

Tube manuals show the tube basing as it would be seen while holding the tube
upside down. All pins are numbered in basing diagrams, with the numbers
reading in a clockwise direction. In some instances, special notations are
made where necessary. For instance, some tubes have an internal shield;
this is indicated because it may be necessary to "ground" the pin to which the
shield is connected.

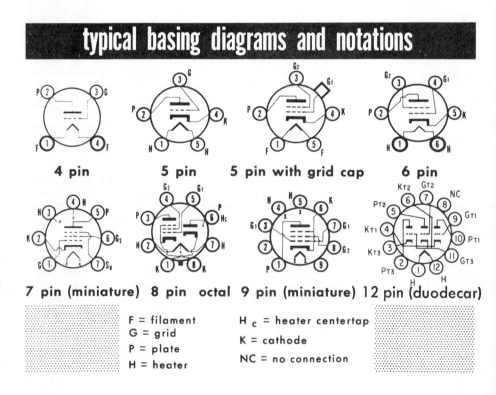

typical basing diagrams and notations

4 pin   5 pin   5 pin with grid cap   6 pin

7 pin (miniature)   8 pin   octal   9 pin (miniature)   12 pin (duodecar)

F = filament   H c = heater centertap
G = grid
P = plate   K = cathode
H = heater   NC = no connection

Electron tubes are classified as diodes, triodes, tetrodes, or pentodes according to the number of elements they contain.

Four important types of electron emission are thermionic, secondary, photoelectric, and cold-cathode.

Oxide-coated materials for cathodes are most commonly used because of their high emission rate.

The important features of a vacuum tube can be seen from its characteristic curves. A number of curves drawn on the same graph are known as a family of curves.

Two types of resistance are present in a diode—d-c and a-c plate resistance.

Static characteristic curves generally show operation with no load or voltage variations in the tube circuit; dynamic characteristic curves generally show operation under load and with voltage variations in the tube circuit.

The purpose of the control grid in triodes is to control the movement of electrons from the space charge to the plate.

Amplification in a triode occurs when a stronger signal is delivered to the output circuit than is received in the input.

An electrostatic field exists between the cathode (space charge) and the control grid in a triode. The direction of this field is such as to pull electrons to the plate when the grid is made positive.

In a triode, the plate is positive with respect to the cathode.

The main advantages of a tetrode over a triode are that it has lower interelectrode capacitance between control grid and plate, and it provides higher amplification.

Plate current saturation is reached when no further increase in plate current occurs as the grid is made more positive.

The main purpose of the screen grid is to reduce interelectrode capacitance between the plate and control grid, thereby preventing self-oscillation.

Pentodes use a suppressor grid to reduce the effects of secondary emission.

Secondary emission occurs when electrons from the space charge strike the plate with sufficient force to dislodge secondary electrons from the plate.

Multi-unit tubes contain more than one set of elements in a single envelope.

REVIEW QUESTIONS

1. Name and explain the action of four important methods of accomplishing electron emission.
2. What is the difference between directly and indirectly heated cathodes?
3. What is emission saturation, and how can it be overcome?
4. Describe the two methods used to control plate current.
5. Explain the difference between static conditions and dynamic conditions when using graphs to illustrate tube characteristics.
6. Describe the action of a diode in rectifying a sine-wave signal.
7. Explain the following tube constants: (a) amplification factor; (b) plate resistance; (c) transconductance.
8. What is the relationship between the value of the plate load and the tube's plate resistance in (a) triode tubes, (b) pentode tubes?
9. Why is there a minimum limit for the plate voltage of a tetrode?
10. What is the purpose of a suppressor grid in a pentode?
11. How does a beam-power tube eliminate the need for a suppressor grid?
12. What is the phase relationship between grid and plate current signals?

Electronic Power Supplies

For the proper operation of radio circuits, various a-c and d-c voltages must be applied to the electron tubes used. As we have seen, the plates and screens of these tubes require d-c voltages — perhaps as much as 400 volts. The heaters or filaments can generally use a-c or d-c voltages, although, as we shall see, a-c voltages are more practical. These voltages may be as high as 117 volts in radio receivers. In certain circuits, the negative d-c

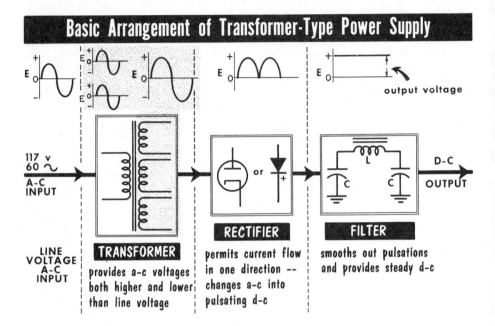

bias applied to the control grids of tubes is supplied by the power supply. In the early days of radio, these voltages were supplied by batteries — an A battery for the filaments, a B battery for the plate and screen voltages, and a C battery for the grid voltage. The modern electronic power supply has eliminated the need for these batteries (except in some portable equipment), and supplies all the necessary voltages required by a radio receiver.

Basically, an electronic transformer-type power supply for radio receivers requires an input of 117-volt 60-hertz a-c, a relatively standard power frequency and voltage. This input is fed into the input of a power transformer which has both step-up and step-down windings. The power transformer supplies a-c voltages to a rectifier — either tube, metallic, or semiconductor. The output of the rectifier feeds into a filter which, in turn, provides a steady d-c voltage output. In addition, various a-c voltages are taken directly from the secondary of the power transformer. The commonly used a-c — d-c or transformerless power supply does not require a power transformer. In normal operation, it is not unusual for the case of a power transformer to run warm, and even slightly hot.

Power Transformers

The purpose of the power transformer is to increase or decrease the a-c input voltage to the values required by the rectifiers and tube heaters of the receivers in use. Usually, the power transformer consists of a primary winding, a high-voltage secondary winding, and a number of low-voltage windings which supply power to the various tube filaments. Since most vacuum tube rectifiers, such as the 5U4, 5Y3, and 5V3, require 5-volt filament voltage, one secondary on most power transformers is rated at 5 volts and 2 or 3 amperes. The ratings of the other filament windings are determined by the number and type of tubes to be heated by this transformer. The most popular heater voltage is 6.3 volts; however, the current rating varies considerably, with popular tube current ratings of 225 ma, 300 ma, and 450 ma. The various heater voltages are obtained through step-down windings from the conventional 117-volt a-c input primary winding.

The high-voltage winding (usually centertapped) is a step-up winding, and commonly provides a-c voltages as high as 800 volts. Many power transformers have an electrostatic shield between the primary and secondary which is bonded to the transformer case; this in turn, is grounded to the receiver chassis. The electrostatic shield prevents high-frequency disturbances in the power line from being fed into the power supply. A current rating is commonly given for the high-voltage secondary winding. For example, a typical power transformer specification might read: "700 volts centertapped at 200 ma, 5 volts at 3 amps, 6.3 volts at 5 amps." Modern power transformers are mounted in steel cases and impregnated.

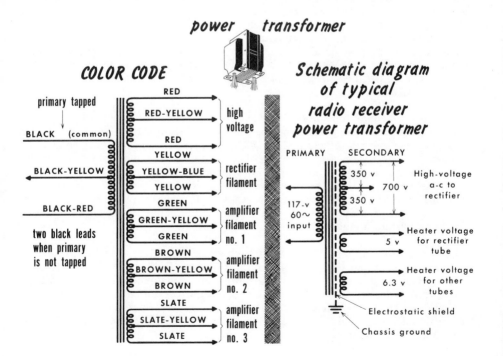

Rectification

RECTIFIERS PROVIDE A LOW-RESISTANCE PATH TO ELECTRON FLOW IN ONE DIRECTION AND A HIGH-RESISTANCE PATH IN THE OTHER DIRECTION

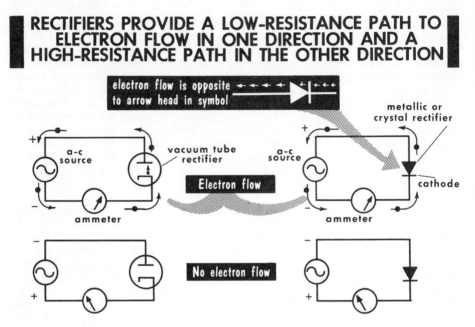

The function of a radio receiver power supply is to provide d-c and a-c voltages for the operation of various circuits. The a-c voltages are obtained directly from the power transformer, which steps up or steps down the line voltage as required by the circuits. The d-c voltages, however, are produced only through a process of rectification and filtering. A rectifier is a device that permits electron flow in one direction and not in another. The rectifier's resistance is very low in one direction and very high in the opposite direction.

The diode vacuum tube makes an excellent rectifier. It permits electron flow from cathode to plate when the plate is positive with respect to cathode and does not permit electron flow when the plate is negative with respect to cathode. Thus, when an a-c voltage is applied across the plate and cathode of a diode vacuum tube, current flows through the tube only during one-half of the a-c cycle. Although this current flow has the waveform of the positive alternation of the a-c voltage, it nevertheless is now direct current — it flows in one direction only. As we shall learn later, the filter smooths these fluctuations into a steady d-c power supply output.

There are other types of rectifiers such as the selenium rectifier. Recent years have seen the growth in popularity of the silicon junction rectifier, a device that has a high ratio of forward-to-back resistance. That is, it offers little resistance to current flow in the opposite direction. The use of a single rectifier permits rectification of half the input cycle. By using more than one rectifier, it is possible to make use of both halves of the input cycle for conversion of a-c to d-c.

Metallic and Semiconductor Rectifiers

The selenium rectifier is a metallic (dry-disc) rectifier. The basic selenium "cell" is limited in the value of voltage and current it can handle. To overcome this limitation, selenium rectifiers consist of stacked cells. Stacking the cells in series increases the value of voltage that can be applied to them; stacking the cells in parallel increases the value of current that can flow from them.

The basic selenium cell consists of a microscopically thin layer of crystalline selenium between two conductors. The supporting plate has the layer of selenium deposited on it, which covers all but the inner and outer edges. The selenium-coated plate is heat treated to form a thin barrier layer. An insulating washer at the center prevents the counter electrode from short-circuiting to the supporting plates.

The action of the barrier layer and selenium is to provide a low-resistance path which readily allows electron flow when the selenium-coated supporting plate (anode) is made positive and the barrier coating of the counter electrode (cathode) is made negative. Reversing the polarities will produce an extremely high-resistance path, providing virtually an open circuit and no current flow. This action is identical to that discussed for diode vacuum tubes.

In addition to selenium rectifiers, the semiconductor action of germanium and silicon (explained in Volume 5) provides diodes capable of handling the voltages and currents used in radio circuits. Practical selenium rectifier stacks can handle applied voltages up to 400 volts (rms), with current ratings as high as 500 ma (or 0.5 ampere).

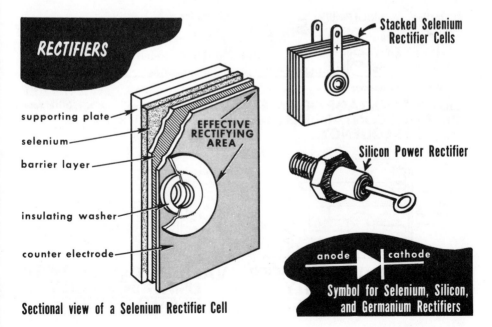

RECTIFIERS

Stacked Selenium Rectifier Cells

supporting plate
selenium
barrier layer
insulating washer
counter electrode

EFFECTIVE RECTIFYING AREA

Silicon Power Rectifier

anode   cathode

Symbol for Selenium, Silicon, and Germanium Rectifiers

Sectional view of a Selenium Rectifier Cell

The Half-Wave Rectifier

The basic circuit to convert a-c to d-c is the half-wave rectifier. The output of the transformer secondary is a sine wave voltage, applied to a load in series with a rectifier. During alternation A, which makes the plate positive, the diode conducts. Current flowing through the load resistor develops an IR or voltage drop which represents the output voltage. During alternation B, which makes the plate negative with respect to the cathode, the diode does not conduct.

The output voltage taken across the load resistor is a pulsating wave of one polarity only. It is called pulsating d-c. The output voltage pulses once for each cycle. The pulses cause the d-c output voltage to be rippled once each cycle, producing a 60-hertz ripple frequency.

Different rectifiers are designed to handle various values of voltages and current. These values determine their ratings. The alternating voltage rating per plate (rms) is the highest value a-c voltage that can be applied between anode and cathode. The peak inverse voltage rating is the maximum voltage that can be applied between anode and cathode when the rectifier is not conducting. The peak inverse voltage of the half-wave rectifier is equal to the peak value across the transformer secondary.

The peak plate current rating in a vacuum tube rectifier represents the maximum value of plate current the cathode can supply. It is an instantaneous value and cannot be handled for any length of time. The load current or output current rating is that value of current which the rectifier can deliver to a load during continuous service.

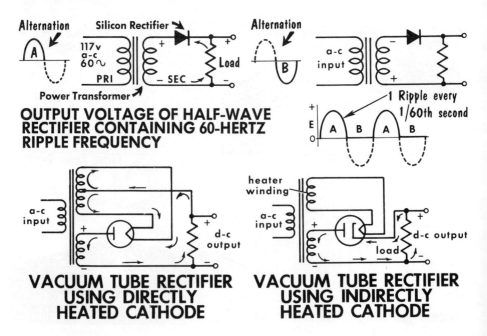

OUTPUT VOLTAGE OF HALF-WAVE RECTIFIER CONTAINING 60-HERTZ RIPPLE FREQUENCY

VACUUM TUBE RECTIFIER USING DIRECTLY HEATED CATHODE

VACUUM TUBE RECTIFIER USING INDIRECTLY HEATED CATHODE

The Full-Wave Rectifier

A full-wave rectifier basically contains two half-wave rectifiers. During alternation A, which places a positive voltage at the anode of diode D1, it conducts. Current flowing through load resistor R1 develops an IR drop which is the d-c output voltage. Diode D2, having a negative voltage at its anode, does not conduct. During alternation B, which places a positive voltage at the anode of diode D2, it conducts. Current flowing through load resistor R2 develops an IR drop which represents the d-c output voltage. Diode D1, having negative voltage at its anode, does not conduct. The output voltage contains two pulses for each cycle, producing a 120-hertz ripple frequency. The average output voltage is higher than that of a half-wave rectifier because the applied a-c voltage is rectified and used for both alternations.

In a practical full-wave rectifier, a single centertapped secondary winding of the transformer replaces the two individual windings. The two load resistors are replaced with one common load resistor. To obtain the same value of output voltage in a full-wave rectifier, each half of the transformer secondary winding has the same value as the single winding used with the half-wave rectifier. The peak inverse voltage rating of a full-wave rectifier is equal to the peak voltage across one half of the secondary winding. Thus, it equals twice that of the half-wave rectifiers.

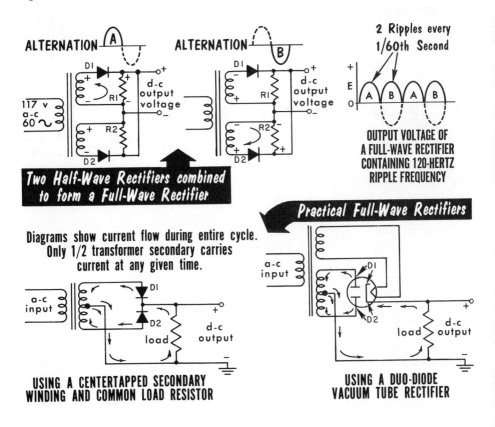

ALTERNATION A   ALTERNATION B   2 Ripples every 1/60th Second

OUTPUT VOLTAGE OF A FULL-WAVE RECTIFIER CONTAINING 120-HERTZ RIPPLE FREQUENCY

Two Half-Wave Rectifiers combined to form a Full-Wave Rectifier

Practical Full-Wave Rectifiers

Diagrams show current flow during entire cycle. Only 1/2 transformer secondary carries current at any given time.

USING A CENTERTAPPED SECONDARY WINDING AND COMMON LOAD RESISTOR

USING A DUO-DIODE VACUUM TUBE RECTIFIER

The Bridge Rectifier

Basically, a bridge rectifier contains two full-wave rectifiers. During alternation A, which places a positive voltage at the anode of diode D2 and a negative voltage at the cathode of D3, they conduct. Current flowing through the load resistor develops an IR drop which represents the d-c output voltage. Diode D1, having a positive voltage at its cathode, and diode D4, having a negative voltage at its anode, do not conduct. Alternation B, which places a positive voltage at the anode of diode D4 and a negative voltage at the cathode of D1, causes them to conduct. Current flowing through the load resistor develops an IR drop which represents the d-c output voltage. Diode D3, having positive voltage at its cathode, and diode D2, having negative voltage at its anode, do not conduct.

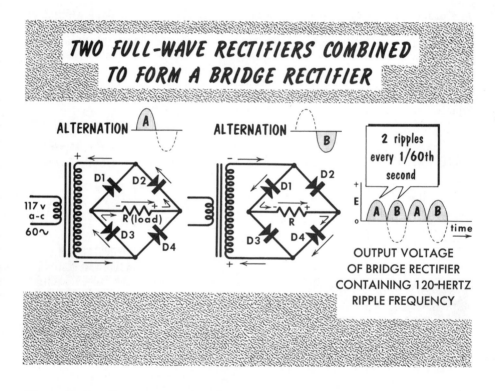

The output voltage, as in the full-wave rectifier, contains two pulses for each cycle, producing a 120-hertz ripple. A bridge rectifier requires only one untapped transformer secondary winding to provide the same value output voltage as the full-wave rectifier. The peak inverse voltage of a bridge rectifier is divided by two rectifiers; thus, it is equal to one-half that of the full-wave rectifier. Bridge rectifiers are used more in transmitter power supplies than in receivers, and will be studied in greater detail later. However, this circuit occasionally is found in receiver power supplies, and it is quite popular in instrument-type a-c rectifiers.

Capacitor Filters

The output of a rectifier (half-wave or full-wave) is not a pure d-c voltage, but a pulsating d-c voltage containing a ripple component. Filter circuits remove the ripple and smooth the voltage to obtain pure d-c. The simplest type of filter is the shunt capacitor connected across the load and rectifier output. We recall that a capacitor opposes any change in voltage across its terminals (in this case, the load) by storing up energy in its electrostatic field whenever the voltage tends to rise, and converting this stored energy back into current flow whenever the voltage across its terminals tends to fall.

Filtering the Output of a HALF-WAVE Rectifier with a Single Capacitor

Filtering the Output of a FULL-WAVE Rectifier with a Single Capacitor

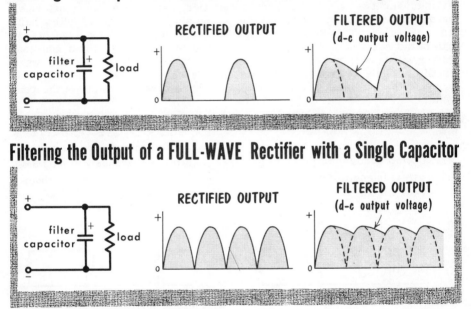

The illustrations show the action of the capacitor filter when either half-wave or full-wave rectifier output voltages are applied to the filter. In both cases, the capacitor charges up to the peak voltage of the rectifier output during the time that current pulses are delivered to the filter and load. When the rectifier output drops off to zero, the capacitor cannot discharge instantaneously; its voltage falls off slowly as it discharges through the load. During the next rectifier current pulse, the capacitor is charged again to the peak voltage, and the cycle is repeated. The only difference between the half-wave and full-wave action is that the capacitor discharges more between current pulses of the half-wave rectifier. Thus, the d-c output voltage of the latter averages less than that of the full-wave rectifier, which almost equals the peak voltage. Because of its poor regulation (large output voltage drops for small load current increases), the simple capacitor filter is not used with rectifiers which supply a large load current.

Capacitor Filters (Cont'd)

It was noted that the peak inverse voltage rating of the half-wave rectifier is equal to the peak value (the rms value x 1.4) across the transformer secondary. This is true with only a resistive load. When using a filter capacitor, the charge on the capacitor is in series with the inverse voltage and doubles the peak inverse voltage applied to the diode. When the diode conducts, the capacitor charges to the peak value (assuming no losses). When the diode rectifier is nonconducting the peak voltage on the capacitor is in series with the peak voltage on the secondary of the transformer and results in a peak inverse voltage that is twice the value of the peak voltage.

In the discussion of the full-wave rectifier we noted that to obtain the same value of output voltage in a full-wave rectifier, each half of the transformer secondary winding has the same value as the single winding used with a half-wave rectifier. This means that in a full-wave rectifier the voltage of that half of the secondary of the transformer that is being applied to a non-conducting diode will be twice that of an equal value of voltage of a half-wave rectifier. This voltage is in series with the charge on the capacitor, thus bringing the total peak inverse voltage to three times the value of the peak voltage.

During conduction the voltage across the capacitor equals the peak voltage

During nonconduction the voltage across the secondary of the transformer is in series with the charge on the capacitor

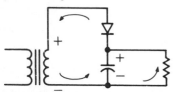

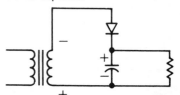

PEAK INVERSE VOLTAGE = 2 X PEAK VOLTAGE

The nonconducting diode has twice the peak inverse voltage value of a nonconducting diode in a half-wave rectifier — Plus the peak voltage across the capacitor

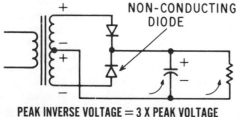

NON-CONDUCTING DIODE

PEAK INVERSE VOLTAGE = 3 X PEAK VOLTAGE

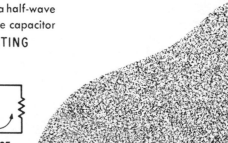

Inductance Filters

The action of a single inductor (choke coil), placed in series with the rectifier output (either half-wave or full-wave), is shown in the illustration. This
filter is usually used in combination with shunt capacitors, as we shall see
later. Essentially, any inductor opposes a change in the amount of current
flowing through it by storing up energy in its magnetic field when the current

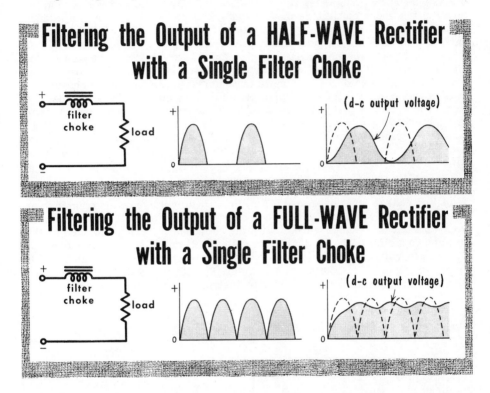

Filtering the Output of a HALF-WAVE Rectifier with a Single Filter Choke

filter choke — load — (d-c output voltage)

Filtering the Output of a FULL-WAVE Rectifier with a Single Filter Choke

filter choke — load — (d-c output voltage)

tends to increase, and by taking energy away from the field to maintain current flow when the voltage across the inductor tends to decrease. Hence, by
placing a choke coil in series with the rectifier and load, changes in the
amount of rectifier output current and output load voltage are minimized.
Another way of examining this action of the series inductor is to consider
that the coil offers a very low resistance (that of the winding alone) to the
passage of d-c, while at the same time offering a high impedance to the passage of fluctuating or alternating currents. The d-c passes through, and the
ripple is largely reduced.

As seen in the output waveforms, the load current through the filter (and,
hence, the load voltage) lags 90° behind the rectifier output voltage, and
never reaches its peak value. The average d-c output voltage from a single
inductor is less than that from the capacitor filter, but the voltage does not
fall off as rapidly with increases in load current as with a capacitor filter.

The Capacitor-Input Filter

Very effective filtering action can be obtained by combining the actions of a shunt capacitor and a series inductor in a capacitance-inductance filter. Various combinations of such filters exist, and in all of them, the action of the capacitors is to resist changes in output voltage by charging and discharging, as required, while the inductors oppose any changes in the amount of the load current by the action of their associated magnetic field. Equivalently, the shunt capacitors may be thought of as forming a low-impedance path from B+ to B- for the ripple voltage, and an essentially infinite impedance to d-c. The series inductors (choke coils) can be considered as offering a low impedance to the passage of d-c and a very high impedance to the ripple current. The typical capacitor-input filter shown in (A) is also called a pi filter, because of its schematic arrangement. An important characteristic of this circuit is its high output voltage at low current drain because the voltage is almost equal to the peak value of the transformer secondary voltage applied to each tube. As the load current increases, the output voltage falls off rapidly and may become less than the effective value of the applied a-c voltage. In other words, we say that the regulation of the capacitor-input filter is poor.

In the circuit shown, the current pulses flowing through the rectifier tubes and filter charge input capacitor C1 up to the peak voltage of the transformer secondary. Between current pulses, the voltage across C1 falls off somewhat, but never reaches zero. With the additional filtering provided by the coil and capacitor C2, the d-c output voltage becomes essentially constant. The ripple voltage may be decreased further by increasing the value of C1, or by adding another filter section as in (B). In general, capacitor-input filters are used when low d-c power is desired, as in radio receivers.

The CAPACITOR-INPUT Filter

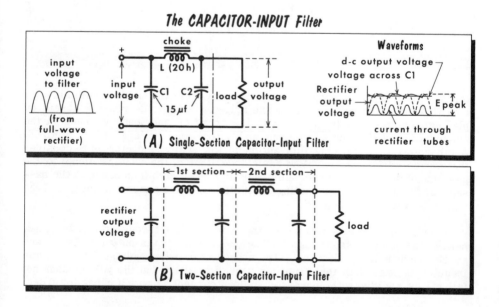

(A) Single-Section Capacitor-Input Filter

(B) Two-Section Capacitor-Input Filter

Choke-Input Filters

The CHOKE-INPUT Filter

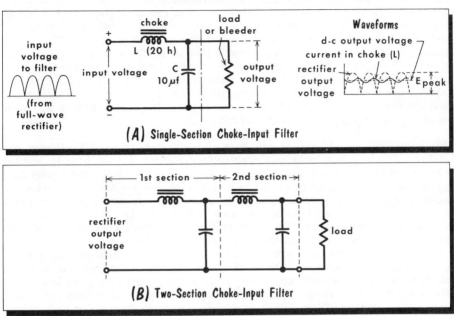

(A) Single-Section Choke-Input Filter

(B) Two-Section Choke-Input Filter

A typical choke-input filter, consisting of a 20-henry series inductor and a 10-microfarad shunt capacitor is shown in (A). When the load draws no current, the d-c output voltage of the choke-input filter is nearly equal to the peak value of the a-c voltage applied to the rectifier, just as in the case of a capacitor-input filter. This is so because, in the absence of a load current, no voltage drop is developed across choke coil L; therefore, output capacitor C charges up to the peak value. However, if even small load current is drawn, the d-c output voltage drops rapidly to some lower value and then remains fairly constant over a wide range of load current values. The initial sharp drop occurs because the series inductor prevents the capacitor from charging to the peak voltage when a load current is drawn. After this initial drop, there is good voltage regulation of the choke-input filter.

The d-c output voltage across C and the load is fairly constant, as shown in the diagram, and its value is somewhat less than the peak a-c voltage, depending upon the load current drawn. The ripple in the d-c load current through the choke can be reduced considerably by increasing the value of the inductance. In some instances, a "swinging choke" is used that varies its inductance according to the load. The inductance of a swinging choke is high at low load currents, and drops off with increasing load currents. As with capacitor-input filters, improved filtering action may be obtained by using a two-section filter shown in (B). Choke-input filters are used whenever the amount of d-c power required is large.

R-C Filters and Bleeder Resistors

When load current requirements are small and a small d-c voltage drop across the filter is permissible, the inductance of a capacitor-input filter may be replaced with a series resistance. The resulting R-C filter is not as effective as an inductive filter, since the series resistor offers as much impedance to d-c as to the ripple voltage. The advantage of the R-C filter is that a resistance is much less expensive than an inductance. In a typical R-C filter, C1 is made sufficiently large to present a very low impedance to the ripple frequency, while at the same time offering practically infinite impedance to d-c. The ripple voltage therefore prefers the shunt path through C1, and the d-c is forced through R, developing a voltage drop across it. Most of the remaining ripple is shunted through C2.

The output voltage of a power supply is often developed across a bleeder resistor. The idea is to achieve better voltage regulation — that is, to prevent changes in current drain in the receiver from changing the power supply output voltage. The bleeder current is a steady continuous drain, lowering the amount of change and providing a steadying effect on the power supply current drain. A bleeder can also be used as a voltage divider by tapping the resistor at different points to provide voltages of different values. Each tap should have a bypass capacitor from the tap to common to prevent interactions between circuits fed by each tap. The bleeder also acts as a safeguard when the receiver is turned off by dissipating the charge stored in the filter capacitors. In addition, when the receiver is turned on, the heaters of the tubes do not warm up immediately, and the circuits draw very little current. The voltage of the power supply may rise to abnormally high values under such no-load conditions, causing component breakdowns. The constant bleeder load prevents this.

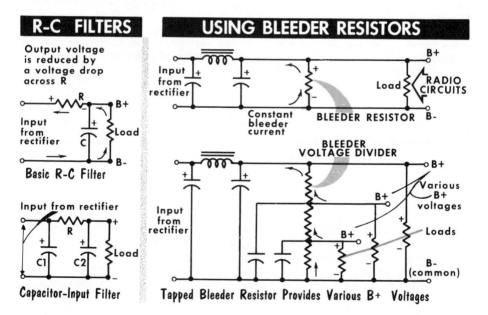

R-C FILTERS

Output voltage is reduced by a voltage drop across R

Basic R-C Filter

Capacitor-Input Filter

USING BLEEDER RESISTORS

Input from rectifier

Constant bleeder current

BLEEDER RESISTOR

BLEEDER VOLTAGE DIVIDER

Tapped Bleeder Resistor Provides Various B+ Voltages

Typical Voltage Divider

A voltage divider connected across the output of a power supply and tapped at a number of points, can provide a selection of different values of output voltage. In the circuit shown, the total output voltage available from the power supply is 250 volts. The maximum output current is 70 ma. Capacitor C1 is the output filter unit, and C2, usually of lower value, provides extra filtering across R2. Load circuit A requires the full 250 volts and draws 40 ma; load circuit B requires only 160 volts and draws 20 ma. Thus, circuits A and B require a total of 60 ma for proper operation. Since the voltage divider or bleeder current should be approximately 10% of the total current, we shall select 10 ma (for convenience) as the bleeder current. Since only 10 ma is to flow through R2, and the voltage required across circuit B is 160 volts, R2 is equal to E/I, or $160/0.01 = 16,000$ ohms. The voltage across R1 must then be 250 volts minus 160 volts, or 90 volts. We know the current through R1 must equal the 10-ma bleeder current plus the 20-ma load current from circuit B, or a total of 30 ma. With this information, we find that the resistance of R1 = E/I, or $90/0.03 = 3000$ ohms.

The total resistance of the voltage divider will then be R1 + R2, or 19,000 ohms. With no loads connected across the voltage divider, the bleeder current through it would be a steady value determined by the resistance of the circuit and the voltage across it. Thus, under no-load conditions, the bleeder current would be I = E/R = $250/19,000 = 13.2$ ma. The power dissipated by R1 would equal E × I, or $90 × 0.03 = 2.7$ watts. To avoid overheating, a resistor having about twice the power rating should be used. In this case, a 5-watt resistor would suffice for R1. Since R2 passes 13.2 ma under no-load conditions, its power rating equals $P = I^2R = 0.0132^2 × 16,000 = 2.79$ watts. Once again, a 5-watt resistor can be used for R2.

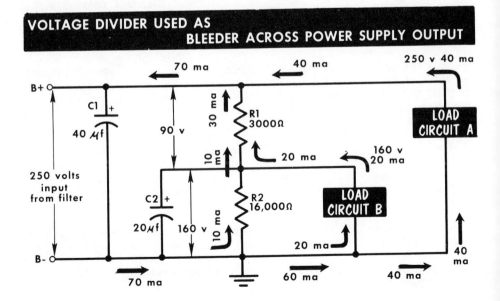

VOLTAGE DIVIDER USED AS BLEEDER ACROSS POWER SUPPLY OUTPUT

Negative Voltage from Power Supplies

So far, in discussing electronic power supplies, we have considered the output to be some voltage that is <u>positive</u> with respect to chassis or ground. In certain instances, it is desirable to have a voltage that is <u>negative</u> with respect to ground, such as when a large negative grid bias is <u>required</u>. In dia-

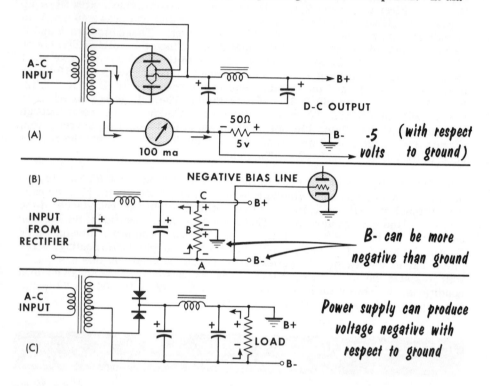

gram A, we see how a negative voltage may be obtained by placing a resistor in series with the centertap lead of a full-wave rectifier. The current passing through the resistor produces a voltage drop that makes the center-tap side negative with respect to ground. This voltage reduces the total amount of B voltage available.

In diagram B, we place a ground tap on the voltage divider or bleeder resistor. Point B, or ground, is positive with respect to A, but negative with respect to C. Thus, in this circuit, B- is actually more negative than ground with respect to B+. The voltage developed between A and B can be applied to a tube as bias voltage.

Diagram C shows how a conventional power supply can be made to provide a negative voltage. By grounding the positive side of the load, all other voltages are negative with respect to this ground. From this, we can see that any power supply can be made to deliver a negative voltage, a positive voltage, or both.

A-C – D-C Power Supplies

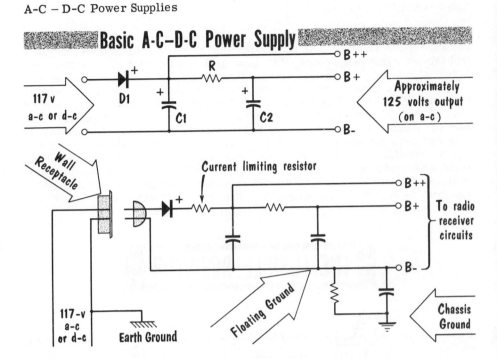

Basic A-C–D-C Power Supply

The popularity of table model radio receivers has led to the development of the economical transformerless power supply. It was found that a simple rectifier circuit could be built that would satisfy the requirements of both an a-c and a d-c line voltage input. With an a-c line input, the circuit becomes a simple half-wave rectifier; with a d-c input, the anode of the diode must be connected to the positive side of the line. The diode then acts merely as a conductor, permitting the dc to be applied directly to the circuits. A capacitor-input R-C type filter is generally used to provide maximum output voltage. Very little trouble is encountered with the 60-hertz ripple or "hum," since these receivers have a poor response at this low frequency. The filter capacitors used have a very high capacitance, usually from 20 to 80 μf. The higher B voltage at the input to the filter can be applied to circuits that do not require a completely ripple-free voltage.

An a-c – d-c filter is potentially dangerous. Notice that one side of the power line is connected directly to the power supply. Thus, if the chassis of the receiver were connected to the "hot" or ungrounded side of the power line, and a person were grounded by a damp floor (by contact with a cold water pipe, radiator, etc.), when he touched the chassis he would actually be placing himself across the power line. To prevent a lethal shock, the negative or B- terminal in these power supplies is isolated from the metal chassis, and is called a floating ground. A capacitor is usually placed between the floating ground and chassis ground to prevent hum pickup. It is often paralleled by a high-value resistance to provide a leakage path for static charges.

The Fusible Resistor

Silicon rectifiers should always be protected from surge overload by a series resistor of low value such as R. An overload may occur as follows: suppose that the a-c cycle is approaching its peak at the instant that the on-off switch is turned on. Also, suppose further, that its polarity is such as to permit current to flow in the forward direction through the silicon rectifier, causing C to charge. Without R in the circuit, the resistance in series with C is very low, so that this capacitor charges almost instantaneously. To bring a capacitor of this size — 100 μf — up to full charge in a very small fraction of a second requires an extremely heavy current, all of which flows through the silicon rectifier. A current of this magnitude flowing through the silicon rectifier even for a short time is very likely to destroy it. The introduction of R into the circuit limits the current to a safe value by increasing the time required to charge the capacitor. Modern receivers use fusible resistors, thus including two protective measures in one component.

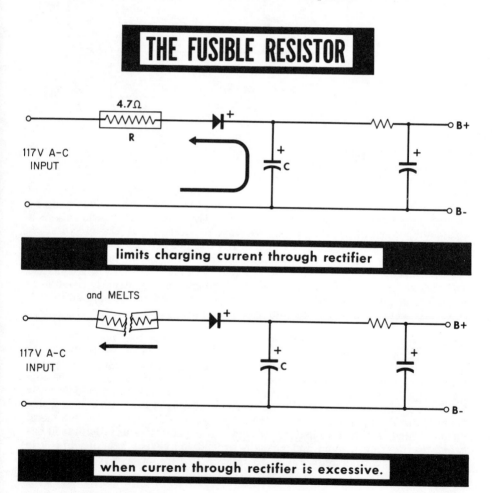

THE FUSIBLE RESISTOR

limits charging current through rectifier

when current through rectifier is excessive.

Half-Wave Voltage Doubler

While radio circuitry can be designed around a wide range of B+ voltages, there are limitations to the quality of sound if the circuits must work from relatively low voltages. Thus, in many receivers, it has become necessary for the circuit designer to make use of a voltage doubler when slightly higher B+ voltages are wanted. A frequently used circuit is shown.

We can see how this circuit operates by assuming that line voltage E is applied to the circuit, with point X being negative with respect to point Y. This

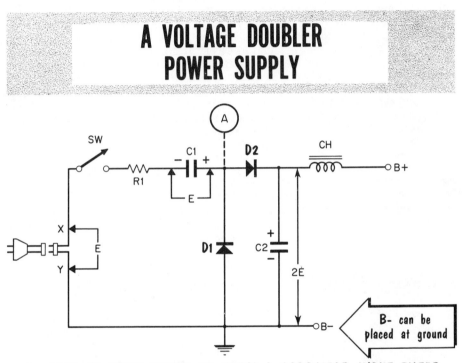

A VOLTAGE DOUBLER POWER SUPPLY

C2 ACTS AS INPUT FILTER TO FORM A CAPACITOR INPUT FILTER

would cause current to flow through the switch, resistor R1, capacitor C1, and rectifier D1, back to point Y. In the process, capacitor C1 would charge approximately to the value of E, as shown. Thus, point A on the diagram would be at E volts with respect to point X. On the next half-cycle, point X would be E volts positive with respect to point Y, or ground. Thus, since point X is E volts positive with respect to ground, and point A is E volts positive with respect to point X, then point A is 2E volts positive with respect to point Y or ground. It is at this time that capacitor C2 can charge up to the full value of point A through rectifier D2. With this voltage doubler arrangement, the difference in potential between B+ and B- is approximately equal to twice that of the input line voltage.

Full-Wave Voltage Doubler

Voltage doublers operate on a-c voltages only. Since they can raise the 117-volt line voltage to approximately 250 volts without the use of a power transformer, they are often referred to as transformerless power supplies. The basic action is to charge two capacitors, each to the peak value of the applied a-c voltage, and to discharge them in series. Assuming a line voltage of 117 volts, the peak value is 1.4 times larger, or 164 volts. With two capacitors in series, each charged to 164 volts, the voltage available becomes 328 volts. With circuit losses, the output voltage averages approximately 250 volts.

During alternation A, the polarity of the voltage applied to the full-wave doubler is such as to have the cathode of diode D2 positive, and the tube does not conduct. The anode of D1 is positive, and it conducts. The current flowing from the negative terminal piles electrons on the negative plate of C1. This drives the electrons off the positive plate of the capacitor through conducting D1 to the positive side of the a-c line. Capacitor C1 charges to the peak value of the applied voltage. On alternation B, the current flows through D2 and charges C2 to the peak value of the applied voltage in the same manner. With C1 and C2 in series, their voltages add. The output voltage will be approximately twice the value of the peak applied voltage. To complete the circuit, additional filters are added. Capacitors C1 and C2 act as the input capacitors, and only the filter choke and output capacitor need to be added. The circuit is called a full-wave doubler. The ripple component is 120 hertz. To ensure that each capacitor receives an equal charge, the capacitors must be alike. A typical value is 20 μf. One side of the 117-volt a-c line is always at ground potential. Because of this, the B- output cannot be placed at ground potential. Doing so will short C2, if the bottom line is grounded, or the entire circuit, if the top line is grounded.

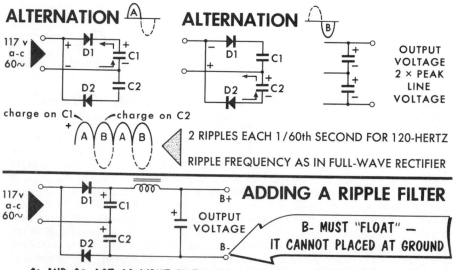

Voltage Quadrupler

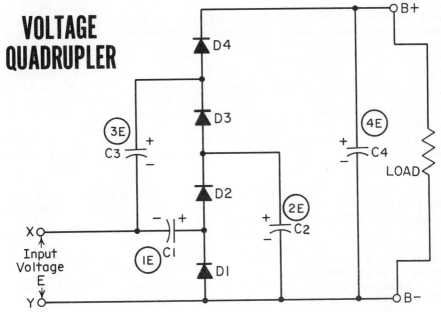

By combining two half-wave voltage doublers a voltage quadrupler circuit is obtained. During the 1st alternation (X-, Y+), D1 conducts to charge C1 to the peak value of the line voltage (E) with the polarities indicated. On the 2nd alternation the negative side of the line (Y) charges C2 with the polarity shown. Diode D2 conducts to add the charge of C1 to that of C2, charging C2 to twice the peak voltage, or 2E. On the 3rd alternation electrons flow from the negative side of the line (X) to charge C3. The charge on C3 is coupled through D3 to place it in series with the charge on C2, causing C3 to be charged to 3E. On the 4th alternation the negative side of the line (Y) will charge C4, which when coupled through D4 is placed in series with the charge on C3. The total charge on C4 is four times the peak value of the line voltage, 4E.

Having reached this steady operating condition, current flow during each half cycle will be only that required to maintain the charge on the capacitors, this in turn is determined by the value of the load. In practice, the quadrupler presents the technical economical limit of voltage multiplication. The regulation becomes progressively poorer and the attained output voltage drops off rapidly with even small load current increases.

The voltage stress across the capacitors becomes increasingly great, requiring costlier units with high-voltage ratings. Also, since the peak current through the rectifier must be limited to the rated values, the possible load current that can be supplied to the rectifiers becomes less with increasing multiplication. Despite these objections, voltage-multiplying circuits using junction diodes are occasionally used for low-current applications.

Heater Circuits for A-C – D-C Receivers

Since a-c–d-c receivers operate directly off the 117-volt power line, special consideration must be given the electrical connections of the tube heaters. By far, the most popular arrangement is the "series string," in which all the tube heaters of a receiver have the same current rating, and are connected in series. An ideal situation was reached when the five-tube a-c–d-c receivers were developed using tubes having heater voltages of 50, 35, 12.6, 12.6, and 12.6 volts, respectively. This totalled 122.8 volts. Connected directly across a 117-volt line, this series string operated very well, with the remaining 5.8 volts being distributed across the various heaters. Actually, this is not critical since most power lines vary slightly in voltage. Throughout the United States, line voltages may range from as little as 110 to as much as 125 volts.

In some series-string heaters, the total voltage required for the heaters may total less than 117 volts. For instance, using a 50C5 (50 volts), 12BA6 (12.6 volts), 12BE6 (12.6 volts), and 12AT6 (12.6 volts) requires a total heater voltage of 87.8 volts. We must then drop 29.2 volts. Using Ohm's law and finding the heater current from a tube manual, we get R = 29.2/0.150 or 195 ohms. In actual practice, a 200-ohm resistor would be used. The power dissipated would equal I^2R, or P = $0.150^2 \times 200$, or 4.5 watts. To protect the receiver completely, a 10-watt resistor should be used. A disadvantage of this heater arrangement is that 4.5 watts are actually being wasted.

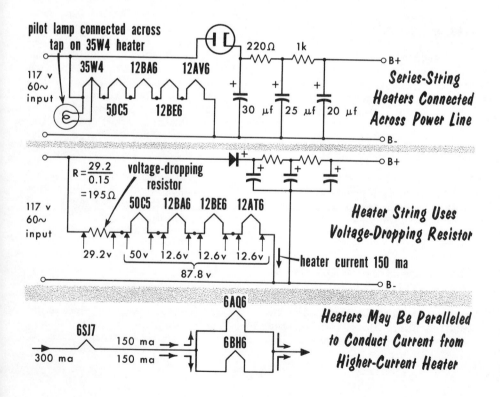

Gas Tube Voltage Regulation

One of the most commonly used voltage regulators is the glow-tube or gaseous-discharge regulator. This is a two-element cold-cathode tube filled with one of the rare gases, such as neon, argon, or helium. Voltage regulator tubes (called <u>VR tubes</u>) are frequently used in power supplies where it is necessary to maintain a constant output voltage in spite of wide changes in load current. The VR-75 (OA3), VR-105 (OB2), and VR-150 (OD3), are examples of these tubes, and provide regulation at specific values of voltage. The VR numbers give the rated <u>constant voltage</u> which occurs across the terminals of each tube for a range of current drain. In actual practice, for example, the OB2 maintains a constant voltage of about 108 volts for current

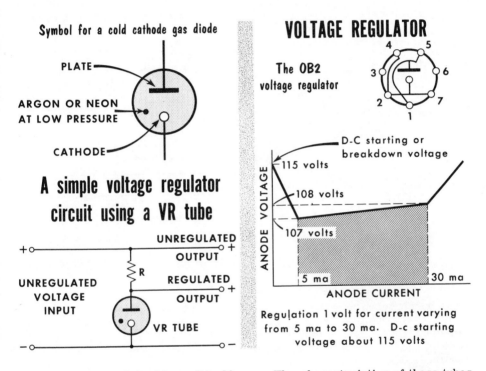

Symbol for a cold cathode gas diode

PLATE

ARGON OR NEON AT LOW PRESSURE

CATHODE

A simple voltage regulator circuit using a VR tube

UNREGULATED VOLTAGE INPUT — R — UNREGULATED OUTPUT + / REGULATED OUTPUT + / VR TUBE

VOLTAGE REGULATOR

The OB2 voltage regulator

D-C starting or breakdown voltage

115 volts
108 volts
107 volts

ANODE VOLTAGE

5 ma   30 ma

ANODE CURRENT

Regulation 1 volt for current varying from 5 ma to 30 ma. D-c starting voltage about 115 volts

variations through it of from 5 to 30 ma. The characteristics of these tubes are determined by the electrode material, the type and pressure of the gas, and the placement and size of the electrodes.

If we look at the plate voltage vs plate current characteristic of the OB2, we notice that there is a slight change in voltage over a wide range of current. This voltage drop is referred to as the <u>regulation of the tube.</u> In the OB2, the regulation is 1 volt over the 5- to 30-ma range. That is, the voltage varies from about 107 to 108 volts. From this characteristic, we see that the internal resistance of the VR tube decreases as the applied voltage increases. This makes it possible for the VR tube to maintain a constant voltage across the load as the load current varies within the rated limits of the VR tube.

Voltage Regulators

The degree of ionization in a VR tube varies with the amount of current flow through it. When a large current flows through the tube, the gas is highly ionized and the internal impedance of the tube is low; when a small current flows, the gas is ionized to a much lesser extent and the tube impedance is high. The product of the current through the VR tube and the internal imped-

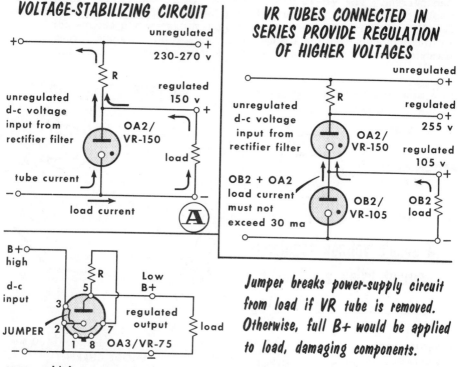

ance, which represents the voltage drop across it, remains practically constant over the operating range. An important requirement in the operation of glow-tube regulators is that a starting voltage somewhat higher than the value of the voltage at which the tube is rated be present across the tube electrodes before the tube will function.

In basic circuit A, a VR tube is connected in series with a resistor R across the output of a filter. Series resistor R limits the current flow through the tube so that its maximum rated value is not exceeded. When the unregulated B+ voltage drops below normal, the voltage across the VR tube drops, the gas in the tube becomes less ionized, the plate resistance increases, and less current flows through the tube and R. The reduced current lowers the IR drop across R, dividing the voltage so that 150 volts is once again across the VR tube. When the applied voltage rises above normal, the VR tube allows more current flow, its plate resistance decreases, and current flow through R increases. This increases the IR drop across R, and the 150 volts across the VR tube maintains a fixed 150-volt drop across it.

Zener Diode Voltage Regulation

The zener diode is similar in appearance to the silicon or germanium rectifier diode. Most often, it is made of silicon and has a very high back resistance. When a reverse voltage is applied to this diode, virtually no reverse
current flows. However, at a certain reverse voltage point, the zener diode
breaks down completely, and the back resistance drops to a very low value.

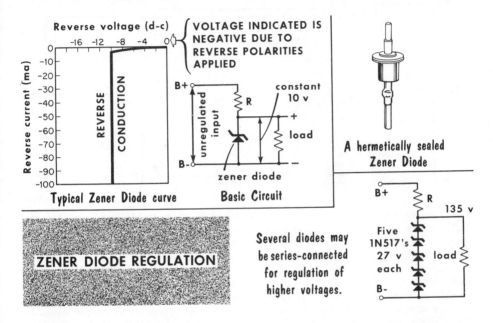

Typical Zener Diode curve   *Basic Circuit*

A hermetically sealed
Zener Diode

ZENER DIODE REGULATION

Several diodes may
be series-connected
for regulation of
higher voltages.

When this occurs, the reverse current increases very rapidly. The effect of
a rapid increase in current, together with a rapid decrease in resistance,
produces an almost constant voltage drop across the diode. Thus, when
biased in a reverse direction, zener diodes can be used as voltage regulators.

Beyond the breakdown or zener voltage, the zener diode exhibits the characteristics of a gas-voltage regulator, and can be considered an equivalent. To
use the zener diode in a VR circuit, positive voltage is applied (through a
series resistor) to the cathode. (This is opposite to the normal application
of voltage to a diode rectifier.) The current flowing through R equals the
sum of the current through the diode plus the load current. When the B voltage drops below normal, the voltage across the diode drops. This increases
the diode resistance, and less current flows through the diode and R. The
reduced current lowers the IR drop across R, dividing the output voltage so
that 10 volts, for example, is again across the diode. When the output voltage
rises above normal, the diode permits more current flow, its resistance decreases, and the current through R increases. This increases the IR drop
across R, and the 10-volt output across the diode is maintained. The load,
connected in parallel across the diode, has a fixed 10-volt drop maintained
across it.

Electron-Tube Regulator

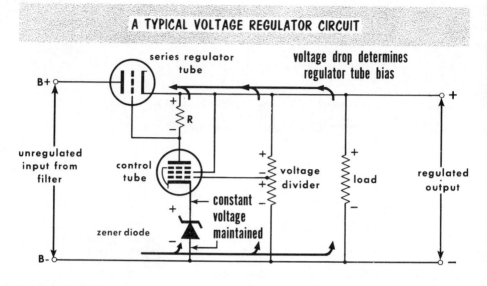

Because an electron tube can be considered as a variable resistor, a very efficient and effective voltage regulator circuit can be built. In the circuit shown, the grid bias of the regulator is obtained by the IR drop across R. Current flows from B- and divides through the load, voltage divider, and through the zener diode, control tube, and R. The total current flows through the regulator tube. The voltage drop across the zener diode maintains a steady voltage on the control tube cathode, and the grid is connected to a voltage divider tap. The grid-cathode voltage of the control tube is equal to the difference between the voltage drop across the zener diode and that across the lower section of the voltage divider. The voltage divider tap is set to provide the proper voltage for biasing the control tube.

If the load voltage tends to rise, either from an increase in the input voltage from the filter or because of a decrease in load current, voltage across the voltage divider and load also rises, as does voltage at the tap of the voltage divider. Voltage at the grid of the control tube thus becomes more positive, with the cathode voltage remaining constant due to the action of the zener diode. The positive-going grid produces an increase in plate current in the control tube which causes a larger IR drop across plate load R, and the grid of the regulator tube becomes more negative. The negative-going grid of the regulator tube increases in its plate resistance and reduces the current flow through the tube. This increases the voltage drop across the regulator tube, and the voltage across the load is reduced to its correct value. When the applied voltage drops below normal, the voltage at the grid of the control tube drops in proportion, reducing plate current in the control tube. The reduced IR drop across R produces a less negative grid bias on the regulator tube. Its plate resistance decreases, and plate current increases. The voltage drop across the regulator tube decreases, and voltage across the load increases to its correct value.

A power transformer usually has a primary winding, a high-voltage secondary winding, and several low-voltage windings which supply the various
tube filaments.

The diode vacuum-tube rectifier allows electron flow from cathode to plate
when the plate is positive with respect to the cathode. When the plate is
negative with respect to cathode, electron flow is retarded.

The peak inverse voltage rating of a rectifier is the maximum voltage that
can be applied when it is not conducting.

The half-wave rectifier is the basic circuit used to convert ac to dc.

Practical full-wave rectifiers use a single, centertapped secondary winding
of the transformer in place of two individual windings.

The output voltage of a full-wave rectifier contains two pulses for each cycle,
producing a 120-hertz ripple frequency.

Capacitance-inductance filters provide very effective filtering action.

Capacitor-input filters are used when the amount of d-c power required is
small; choke-input filters are used when the d-c power requirement is
large.

For better voltage regulation, a bleeder resistor is used to prevent receiver
current drain changes from changing the power supply output voltage.

In a-c – d-c receiver power supplies, a floating ground is used to prevent a
lethal shock by isolating the B- terminal from the metal chassis.

Voltage doubler and voltage quadrupler circuits can be obtained by charging
series-connected capacitors.

Voltage-regulator tubes are frequently used in power supplies where it is
necessary to maintain a constant output voltage despite wide load current
changes.

The degree of ionization in a VR tube varies with the amount of current flow
through it.

Zener diodes have a very high back resistance, but at a certain reverse voltage point, they break down and the back resistance drops to a very low
value.

REVIEW QUESTIONS

1. Describe the operation of a half-wave rectifier; of a full-wave rectifier.
2. What is the output voltage ripple frequency of a half-wave rectifier? Of
   a full-wave rectifier?
3. What are the advantages and disadvantages of gas-filled rectifier tubes?
4. Describe the operation of a bridge rectifier using selenium rectifiers.
5. How are capacitor-input and choke-input filters used in relation to d-c
   power requirements?
6. What are the advantages of using a bleeder resistor in a power supply?
7. Describe the action of a full-wave voltage doubler; a half-wave voltage
   doubler.
8. What are the disadvantages of a voltage quadrupler?
9. Why is a floating ground used in an a-c — d-c power supply circuit?
10. What property of a gas-filled tube enables it to be used as a voltage
    regulator?
11. Describe the action of a zener diode used as a voltage regulator.
12. Describe the action of a series regulator tube.

Amplification

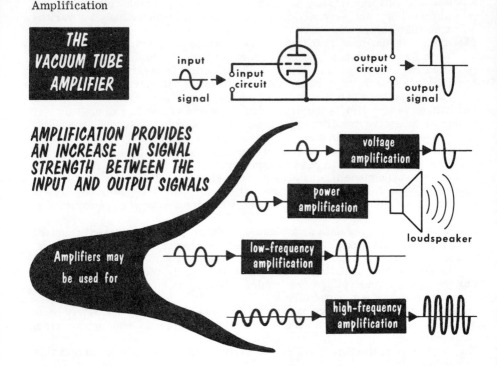

We have studied the use of the electron tube as a rectifier in power supply
circuits. Now, we shall study the electron tube in its most important application – that of an amplifier. The more common expression "vacuum tube"
will be used, since all electron tubes used for amplification of electrical signals are of the vacuum type. It is the use of the vacuum tube as a device
for amplification that has made radio broadcasting and communications possible.

There are many ways of classifying amplifiers. In each instance, the vacuum tube itself must not be thought of as the complete amplifier, but rather
as an amplifying device which, together with appropriate associated circuitry,
can produce an amplified version of the input signal in its output circuit.
Vacuum tube amplifiers are often classified in various categories according
to the type of operation. Generally, however, there are two classifications
that are most commonly accepted. The first is in terms of voltage and
power. Voltage amplifiers are designed to receive small input voltages and
to put out large-amplitude versions of the input signal. Power amplifiers
are designed to deliver into their output circuit signal power that can be used
by a special device, such as a loudspeaker or an antenna circuit in a transmitter. The second popular classification of amplifiers is in terms of
frequency. The general grouping here is low frequency and high frequency.
We shall study the differences in tubes and tube circuitry when we amplify
low- and high-frequency signals. To begin our study, we shall return to our
discussion of vacuum tube characteristics.

Dynamic Characteristics of the Triode

Thus far, we have not seen a triode do any useful work. We have varied the voltages applied to the grid and plate of the tube, and have observed the amount of plate current flowing through the tube to the plate, and from there, through the external circuit and back to the cathode. But we have not seen any results that this current has produced. In fact, we have only studied the behavior of a triode under <u>static</u> conditions and have developed a number of interesting families of characteristics, which up to now have served no useful purpose. In order that a vacuum tube be of any practical use, a <u>load resistance</u> must be inserted in its plate circuit. Once a load resistance is present, the plate current will develop a voltage drop across it which may be transferred to the input of another tube, or the tube can be used directly to do useful work. If an input signal is applied to the grid of a tube the plate current will create an amplifier version of this signal — or output signal — across such a load resistor.

The presence of a load resistor in the plate circuit of a triode gives rise to the so-called <u>dynamic characteristics</u> of a tube, which are the actual conditions of operation used in practice, and hence, far more important than the static characteristics we have studied. The dynamic characteristics are thus a graphical portrayal of tube behavior under load. We have illustrated a basic triode circuit with a load inserted into the plate circuit, assigning typical values to the plate voltage and load resistor. For comparison, the same circuit is shown without a load.

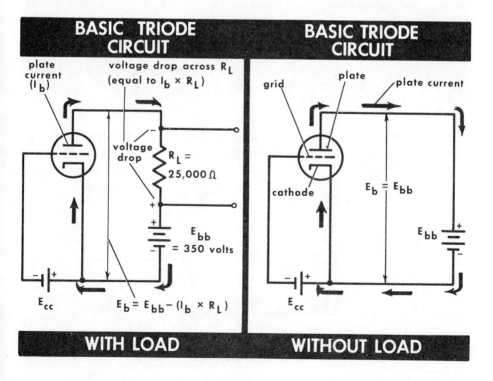

BASIC TRIODE CIRCUIT

plate current (I_b)

voltage drop across R_L (equal to $I_b \times R_L$)

voltage drop

$R_L = 25,000\ \Omega$

$E_{bb} = 350$ volts

E_{cc}

$E_b = E_{bb} - (I_b \times R_L)$

WITH LOAD

BASIC TRIODE CIRCUIT

grid

plate

plate current

cathode

$E_b = E_{bb}$

E_{bb}

E_{cc}

WITHOUT LOAD

Voltage Drop across Load

The load resistor R_L is in series with the plate supply voltage E_{bb} and the tube itself. Consequently, the electrons on their way back to the tube's cathode must flow through this load resistor and develop a voltage drop across it. This is known as the output voltage E_{RL}. By Ohm's law, since $E = I \times R$, the voltage drop across R_L (E_{RL}) is then $I_b \times R_L$. You remember that the sum of the voltage drops around a series circuit must equal the source voltage. Evidently, then, the plate voltage supply E_{bb} must equal the sum of the plate-to-cathode voltage E_b, plus the voltage drop across the load resistor E_{RL}. In other words, the plate voltage across the tube is the difference between the plate supply voltage E_{bb} and the voltage drop across E_{RL} (equal to $I_b R_L$). This is a very important relationship to remember. It shows that the plate voltage (E_b) decreases as the plate current increases, since the plate supply voltage E_{bb} and the load resistor R_L are both fixed in value. This is the main difference between the static condition of operation, where the plate voltage equals the plate supply or battery voltage ($E_b = E_{bb}$), since no load is present, and the dynamic condition of operation with a load, where the plate voltage is the difference between the plate supply voltage and the voltage drop across the load $\left[E_b = E_{bb} - (I_b R_L)\right]$.

As an example, imagine first that E_{cc} is adjusted to such a high negative value as to cut off I_b. With no plate current flow, there is no voltage drop across R_L, and the plate voltage equals E_{bb} or 350 volts. Now assume that the bias is changed to permit 1 ma of plate current to flow through the plate circuit. We find that the plate voltage now is 350 - (0.001 × 25,000), or 325 volts. In this case, the voltage drop across R_L is relatively low, and the internal drop across the plate resistance is high (325 volts). Imagine now that the grid bias is adjusted to a less negative value, to allow as much as 12 ma of plate current to flow through the circuit. The plate voltage is now 350 - (0.012 × 25,000), or 50 volts. For this operating condition, we see that most of the voltage drop appears across R_L, and very little across the internal resistance of the tube.

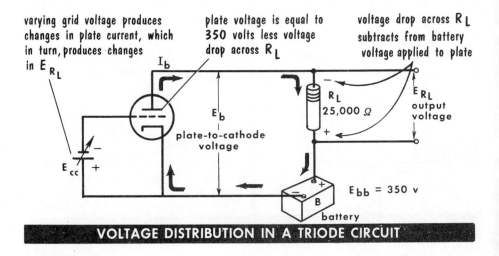

varying grid voltage produces changes in plate current, which in turn, produces changes in E_{R_L}

plate voltage is equal to 350 volts less voltage drop across R_L

voltage drop across R_L subtracts from battery voltage applied to plate

I_b

E_b
plate-to-cathode voltage

R_L 25,000 Ω

E_{RL} output voltage

E_{cc}

E_{bb} = 350 v

battery

VOLTAGE DISTRIBUTION IN A TRIODE CIRCUIT

The Load Line

The effect of a plate load connected in a triode circuit can be predicted in advance. A graphical representation of the load, known as a load line, can be added to the static plate characteristics of the tube. The load line shows the voltage distribution of the plate supply voltage, the voltage across the load, and the plate voltage for different values of plate current and grid voltage. The load line is usually constructed by joining two points – one on the plate-current axis (corresponding to zero plate voltage), the other on the plate-voltage axis. This point corresponds to a condition when the tube is at cutoff (zero plate current), and the entire plate supply voltage E_{bb} equals the plate voltage. The point on the plate-current axis corresponds to the current flow when the entire plate supply voltage is the voltage drop across the load, resulting in zero plate voltage.

For a typical triode tube using a 25,000-ohm plate load and a plate supply of 350 volts, a typical load line can be drawn on the same graph as the static plate characteristics of the tube. The point on the plate-voltage axis is the 350-volt plate supply voltage (zero plate current). Location on the point on the plate-current axis requires the use of Ohm's law. The plate supply voltage (350 volts) is the theoretically maximum voltage drop across this 25,000-ohm resistor. Ohm's law is used to find the value of the plate current:

$$I = E/R = 350/25,000 = 14 \text{ ma}$$

The second point is then marked at the intersection of 0 volts and 14 ma. Using a straight edge, a line is drawn connecting the two intersections; this line is the load line.

25,000-Ohm Load Line Constructed on a Plate Family of Curves

zero plate voltage
(full plate supply
voltage dropped
across R_L)

$I_b = \dfrac{350}{25,000}$
$= 0.014$ amp

$E_{cc} = 0 \text{ v}$, -2 v, -4 v, -6 v, -8 v, -10 v, -12 v, -14 v, -16 v, -18 v

$E_{bb} = 350 \text{ v}$

$R_L = 25,000 \text{ ohms}$

LOAD LINE

PLATE CURRENT (MA)

maximum plate voltage
(plate supply voltage)

PLATE VOLTAGE (VOLTS)

Using the Load Line

A load line can be used to find the value of plate voltage for a specific value of plate current, or the value of plate current for a specific value of grid voltage. For example, with a grid voltage of -6 volts, we check its intersection with the load line and find that the plate voltage is 190 volts and the plate current 6.4 ma.

We can go further, and observe plate current and voltage during a complete cycle of input voltage. With the triode biased at -6 volts, a 2-volt peak input voltage swings the grid bias up to -4 volts and down to -8 volts. Projecting toward the plate current axis, we see that during this time, plate current rises from 6.4 ma at -6 volts bias, to approximately 7.6 ma at -4 volts bias, and decreases to 5.2 ma at -8 volts bias. At the same time, the plate voltage moves from 190 volts at -6 volts bias down to 160 volts at -4 volts on the grid, and up to 220 volts at -8 volts on the grid. Thus, we see a remarkable thing. By use of the load line, we have a "picture" of plate voltage and plate current variations at every instant of the input cycle. For any given grid voltage variation, we can predict plate current and plate voltage variations. We thus "see" the dynamic operation of a tube under a given set of conditions. For different values of load resistance, the load line would take different positions, and the same input voltage would produce different plate current and plate voltage variations.

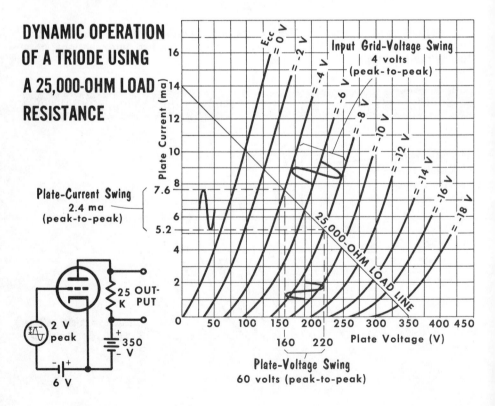

DYNAMIC OPERATION OF A TRIODE USING A 25,000-OHM LOAD RESISTANCE

Input Grid-Voltage Swing
4 volts
(peak-to-peak)

Plate-Current Swing
2.4 ma
(peak-to-peak)

Plate-Voltage Swing
60 volts (peak-to-peak)

Dynamic Transfer Characteristics

Although the load line is very important when it is added to the static plate family, it does not tell the story of dynamic operation as conveniently as does the static grid family with the effect of the load superimposed. If this is done, the resulting plate-current, grid-voltage characteristic is known as the dynamic transfer characteristic. We show the static plate family with the 25,000-ohm load line and the static grid family, but with the dynamic characteristic added. Although this dynamic curve can be developed directly by the appropriate measurements, we have taken the easy way of simply transposing the information onto the static grid family. Both figures have a common plate current (vertical) axis, but the horizontal axis for A is the grid voltage, while for B, it is the plate voltage. It is, therefore, simply necessary to plot the plate current values for any particular grid voltage from the load line of B onto the corresponding plate-current, grid-voltage points of the graph in A. Thus, we obtain the dynamic transfer characteristic for a 25,000-ohm load.

Notice that the dynamic characteristic is much less steep and less curved than the static plate-current, grid-voltage curves. The insertion of a load in the plate circuit has resulted in straightening out the static characteristics, and has made them more linear than before. This is important in relation to the amount of distortion that occurs during operation.

CONSTRUCTION of DYNAMIC TRANSFER CHARACTERISTIC
from PLATE and GRID FAMILIES of CURVES (Using 25,000-ohm load)

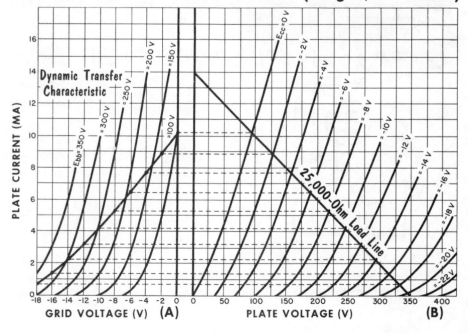

Plate Voltage and Current Components

Thus far, we have considered the fundamental triode circuit operated with d-c potentials, although we have, on occasion, varied these potentials in a more or less mechanical manner to observe the effect on the plate current. In most applications, however, the triode is operated with an alternating voltage (usually called the exciting or signal voltage) applied to the grid circuit, in addition to the d-c grid bias voltage. The effect of this is to vary the grid-to-cathode voltage of the tube and cause a corresponding variation in the plate current. The plate current variations, in turn, generate a varying voltage across the load resistor, the so-called output voltage of the tube. In order to understand this dynamic amplifying process, we shall have to modify our thinking toward an alternating-current viewpoint of the triode tube. Actually, the triode is no different from the diode in that it is capable of passing a current in only one direction, from cathode to plate, and only when the plate is positive with respect to the cathode. Hence, the varying plate current and voltages of the tube are all unidirectional, and they never reverse to negative polarity.

The proper way to consider the varying plate current and voltages, with a grid signal voltage present, is to imagine them composed of two components. One component is the d-c or quiescent value of the current or voltage for a fixed grid bias, with no signal voltage present in the grid circuit. Superimposed on this d-c component is a second component of the current or voltage under consideration, namely, the varying or alternating component caused by the exciting voltage or signal in the grid circuit of the tube. This last point is important and often misunderstood. The flow of plate current is direct current. However, because it rises and falls about a center or zero signal value, it has an a-c component. Frequently, current of this type is referred to as pulsating dc.

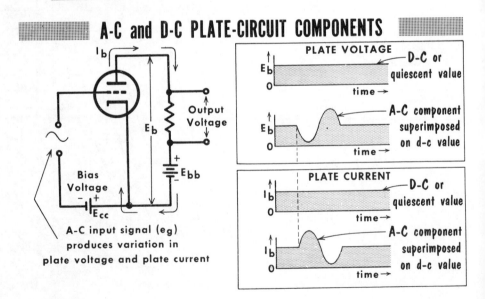

A-C and D-C PLATE-CIRCUIT COMPONENTS

A-C input signal (eg) produces variation in plate voltage and plate current

Grid Bias

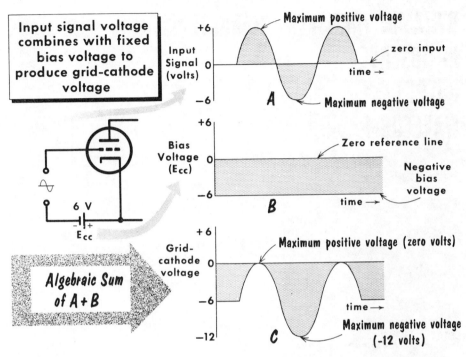

Input signal voltage combines with fixed bias voltage to produce grid-cathode voltage

Input Signal (volts)

A — Maximum positive voltage / zero input / time → / Maximum negative voltage

6 V
E_{cc}

Bias Voltage (E_{cc})

B — Zero reference line / Negative bias voltage / time →

Algebraic Sum of A + B

Grid-cathode voltage

C — Maximum positive voltage (zero volts) / time → / Maximum negative voltage (-12 volts)

We have seen that the a-c signal voltage is inserted in <u>series</u> with the grid bias battery E_{cc}. The reason for this is simple. In its basic application as an amplifier of tiny signal voltages, the triode is operated to consume no power in the grid circuit, because generally, no power is available from the extremely weak radio signals. This is one of the features of a tube – it can be purely voltage operated in the grid circuit, although power may be available from the plate circuit. To consume no power in the grid circuit, it is essential that no grid current flow. To avoid the flow of grid current, the tube must be operated at a negative grid voltage, or at least at a voltage which never rises above zero to positive values, since under those conditions, grid current would flow and power would be consumed.

This is the real purpose of the negative grid bias – to prevent the control grid voltage from ever rising to positive values which results in grid-current flow. We show an a-c sine-wave signal voltage for grid excitation which rises to a positive peak of +6 volts, and has a negative peak of -6 volts. In series with this a-c voltage, we have applied a d-c grid bias of -6 volts. (From now on, we shall always reserve the term <u>bias</u> for the d-c grid voltage.) The total instantaneous voltage acting between grid and cathode of the tube (e_c) is the <u>algebraic sum</u> of the a-c signal voltage and the d-c grid bias. The bias voltage of -6 volts has been represented by a straight line, 6 volts below the zero-voltage reference line. Note that at no time does the grid swing positive with respect to the cathode.

Operating Point

DYNAMIC TRANSFER CHARACTERISTIC is used
to OBSERVE
OUTPUT
WAVEFORM

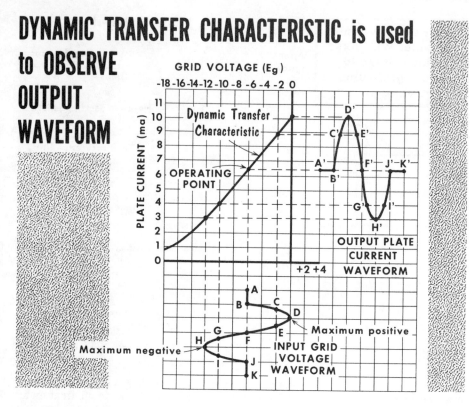

To demonstrate the method of predicting the plate-current behavior from the dynamic transfer characteristic, it is necessary first to establish an operating point on the characteristic curve. This is determined by the amount of fixed grid bias applied to the tube. The bias establishes a steady value of plate current which exists for a zero-input signal voltage, and is generally referred to as the quiescent or d-c value of plate current. In the diagram, we have repeated the dynamic transfer characteristic for our typical triode with a 25,000-ohm load resistor and 350-volt plate supply voltage. This curve portrays graphically the variations in output plate current produced with a varying input grid voltage. The curve actually shows the behavior of the plate circuit for a given input signal voltage and a fixed operating point.

If we use -6 volts for the operating point, the a-c signal having a positive peak of +6 volts will not drive the grid positive; hence, no grid current is drawn. With -6 volts bias, corresponding to zero voltage input, we obtain a plate current of 6.4 ma from the dynamic characteristic. By plotting the input grid voltage swing against the curve, and then projecting point by point to the plate current axis, we obtain a pattern of the plate current waveform. Since the plate current flows through R_L, the voltage drop across R_L is an accurate reproduction of the grid input voltage.

Linearity of Output Waveform

For low distortion and a faithful reproduction of the input waveform, the plate current changes must be linear; that is, they must be directly proportional to the grid voltage changes. If we examine the dynamic transfer characteristic, we see that it is quite linear over the major portion; however, the lower left-hand portion curves somewhat and is not linear. On the preceding page, we projected the input grid voltage against the linear portion of the curve and thus obtained an exact replica of the input grid voltage in the form of the output plate current waveform. We shall now move our operating point down to -12 volts. In so doing, the input grid voltage reaches a maximum positive value of -6 volts, and a maximum negative value of -18 volts. In addition, we see that to the left of the operating point, the grid voltage is projected against the nonlinear portion of the curve.

When we make a point-by-point projection, it can be seen that the curvature of the dynamic transfer characteristic has produced a distorted output plate current waveform, with the negative peak flattened out. This flattening represents signal distortion. Thus, by properly locating the operating point on the linear portion of the dynamic transfer characteristic (keeping in mind the peak-to-peak swing of the input grid voltage), the output plate current waveform can be made an exact replica of the input grid voltage.

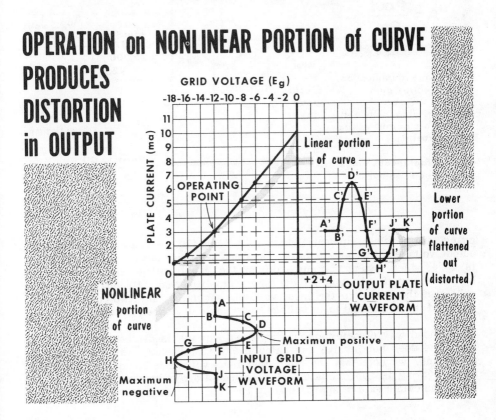

OPERATION on NONLINEAR PORTION of CURVE PRODUCES DISTORTION in OUTPUT

Calculating Amplification

We have not yet shown how much the simple triode amplifier has amplified the input signal voltage in the grid circuit. Although our plate current waveform looks bigger than the grid voltage waveform, this is no indication of the amount of amplification, since we cannot compare the amplitude of a current with that of a voltage. To obtain the correct amplification, we must compare the output voltage developed as a result of the drop across R_L with that of the input or signal voltage applied to the grid. Hence, we can define the amount of voltage amplification, also known as voltage gain, as the ratio of the output voltage to the input voltage.

You will note that the equation deals strictly with instantaneous values of a-c quantities. There are two ways we can determine the output voltage (e_{out}). One way is to multiply the a-c plate current (i_p) by the load resistance (R_L); in other words, the a-c voltage across the load ($e_{out} = i_p \times R_L$). In our example, the plate current rises from its quiescent or d-c value of 6.4 ma for zero signal to a maximum of 10.1 ma for the 6-volt positive peak of the a-c input signal. The peak value of the a-c plate current (i_p), then, is the total

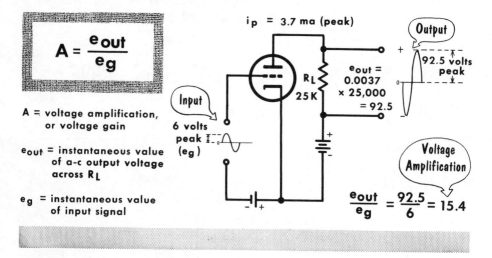

$$A = \frac{e_{out}}{e_g}$$

A = voltage amplification, or voltage gain

e_{out} = instantaneous value of a-c output voltage across R_L

e_g = instantaneous value of input signal

i_p = 3.7 ma (peak)

Output

Input

6 volts peak (e_g)

R_L 25K

e_{out} = 0.0037 × 25,000 = 92.5

92.5 volts peak

Voltage Amplification

$$\frac{e_{out}}{e_g} = \frac{92.5}{6} = 15.4$$

change in the plate current, which is 3.7 ma (10.1 - 6.4 = 3.7). The peak output voltage value is 92.5 volts. Thus, we see that the voltage amplification is 15.4, which means that any value of the input voltage will be multiplied by a factor of 15.4 because of the tube's amplification. (We have used peak values of the output to the input voltage. Actually, any two corresponding points of the output and input voltage wave could have been compared.)

The second way of determining the output voltage is directly from the load line, and does not involve any calculations whatsoever. Referring back to page 3-60, we note that the peak grid input voltage is 2, and the peak plate voltage swing is approximately 30. Hence, a direct reading from the graph would indicate a gain of approximately 15.

Current and Voltage Phase Relationships

PHASE RELATIONSHIPS IN TRIODE AMPLIFIER

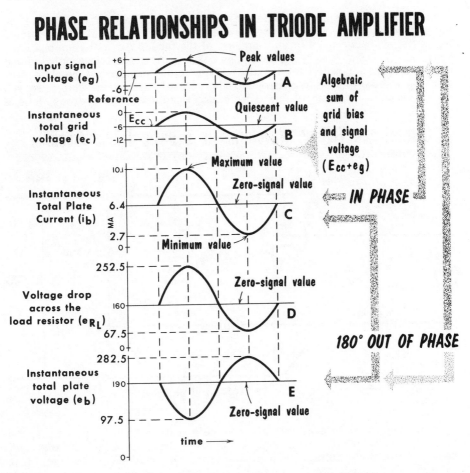

We have seen how the signal applied to the grid of a triode is amplified by the tube, causing a magnified reproduction of the input signal to appear in the output (plate circuit). We have shown further, that the plate current – hence, the output voltage – faithfully duplicates the input signal waveform, provided that the operating point of the tube is properly chosen. We have not yet considered the timing, or relative phase, between the various input and output voltages and currents.

We see five sine waves which depict the phase relationships in a triode amplifier circuit. Our previous example for -6 volts bias, 350 volts plate supply, and 25,000 ohms load resistance has been chosen again for continuity, but the phase relations are true regardless of the particular values of the voltages and currents. The dashed vertical lines passing through the waveforms compare corresponding points at the same instant in time for each of the waveforms.

Current and Voltage Phase Relationships (Cont'd)

As you can see, the phase relations are entirely different for waveform E on the preceding page, which represents the instantaneous total plate voltage (e_b), existing between plate and cathode of the tube. You will remember the equation $e_b = E_{bb} - i_b R_L$, which shows that for a fixed plate supply voltage (E_{bb}), the instantaneous total plate voltage (e_b) decreases as the plate current (i_b) and the total voltage drop across the load, increase. This is so, you recall, because with increasing plate current and load voltage drops, less of

Current and Voltage Waveforms in a Basic Triode Amplifier

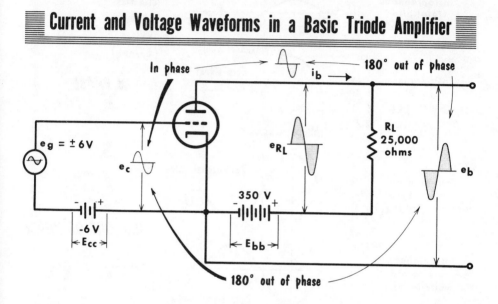

the supply voltage is available at the tube's plate. On the other hand, the lower the plate current, the smaller is the voltage drop across the load; hence, more plate voltage is left over from the fixed supply voltage. It is evident, therefore, that the total plate voltage is in an opposing or out-of-phase relation to the plate current and the input signal. This is brought out by the shape of curve E.

From page 3-60, we see that the quiescent value of the plate voltage (for zero signal) is 190 volts for a bias of -6 volts and a load of 25,000 ohms. When the grid voltage rises to 0 volts for a signal of +6 volts, the plate voltage falls to a minimum value of 97.5 volts, while the drop in grid voltage to -12 volts for a signal of -6 volts produces a rise in total plate voltage to its maximum value of 282.5 volts. Thus, whenever the signal voltage, e_g, is at its maximum positive value, the plate voltage e_b is at its minimum value, and vice versa. It appears as if the plate voltage has been shifted by one half-cycle, or 180° with reference to the grid voltage. We can conclude by stating that the plate current is in phase with the grid voltage, but the plate voltage is 180° out of phase with the grid voltage. This is generally true for all types of vacuum tubes that have a control grid.

Interelectrode Capacitances

Although it appears at first glance that all the electrodes in a triode tube are well isolated from each other, and that they cannot influence each other except through the flow of plate current, this is not quite correct. You remember that we discussed the electrostatic fields existing between the charged electrodes of a triode, such as the fields between plate and cathode, plate and grid, and grid and cathode. You may also recall from elementary electricity that an electrostatic field between any two charged metal plates is the equivalent of an electrical capacitor capable of holding a certain charge. Thus it is evident that definite capacitances exist between all the metal electrodes of a triode which, however tiny, do affect the operation of a tube.

The illustration indicates the capacitances existing between the metal electrodes — the so-called interelectrode capacitances. The most important of these is the capacitance between the control grid and the plate of the tube. There is also capacitance between the control grid and cathode and between the plate and the cathode. The values of these capacitances are very small, generally in the order of 2 to 10 μμf. At low audio frequencies (between 20 and 15,000 hertz), the effect of these tiny capacitances is almost negligible.

CAPACITANCE EXISTS BETWEEN the ELEMENTS of a TUBE

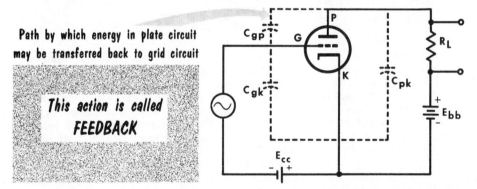

Path by which energy in plate circuit may be transferred back to grid circuit

This action is called
FEEDBACK

But at higher radio frequencies (from 100 kHz up), when their reactance becomes low, they play an important role in influencing the tube's operation. The capacitance between grid and plate may have the very undesirable effect of coupling the output (plate) circuit back to the input (grid) circuit, resulting in the feedback of energy from plate to grid.

As we shall learn later in our study of oscillators, energy feedback is useful. However, the feedback of energy as a result of interaction between the grid and the plate circuits in an amplifier frequently presents serious problems in achieving circuit isolation. A reduction of interelectrode capacitances by the additional shielding of electrodes is achieved in multi-electrode tubes, such as the tetrode and pentode. Without this shielding, there would still be undesirable coupling and feedback effects between the plate and grid circuits.

Class-A Operation

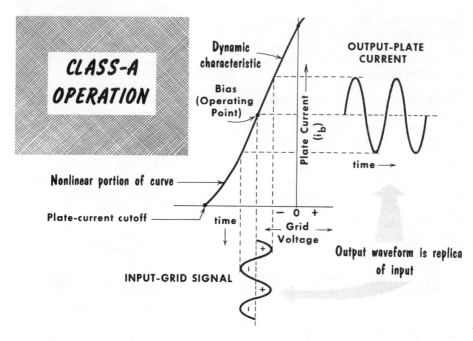

The position of the quiescent or operating point on the dynamic transfer characteristic, established by the d-c grid bias voltage, determines the different classes of operation of an amplifier. These are: Class-A, -B, -AB, and -C. In radio receivers, the most commonly used class of operation is Class-A. In a Class-A amplifier, the grid bias is such that plate current flows in the output circuit during 360° of the input grid voltage cycle. In short, in a Class-A amplifier, plate current flows continuously. Minimum distortion of the output waveform takes place because Class-A amplifiers are generally small-signal low-power units in which the entire operation takes place over the linear portion of a tube's dynamic characteristic. At no time does the grid go positive under normal operating conditions, nor does it swing into the nonlinear portion of the curve on its negative cycle.

Should the control grid go positive on the positive half of the input cycle, part of the input grid signal would be lost or clipped, and the positive half of the output plate current waveform distorted. Similarly, should the negative half of the input grid signal swing beyond the plate current cutoff point, plate current would stop flowing and the negative half of the output plate current waveform would be clipped, with accompanying distortion. In most instances, the operating point of a Class-A amplifier is in the center of the linear portion of the dynamic characteristic at about one-half plate current cutoff value. In terms of plate efficiency, which can be defined as the ratio of a-c power output developed across R_L to the d-c power supplied to the plate, Class-A amplifiers are quite inefficient. They run as low as 20% or less, due to the high average value of plate current and, consequently, high plate power dissipation.

Class-B Operation

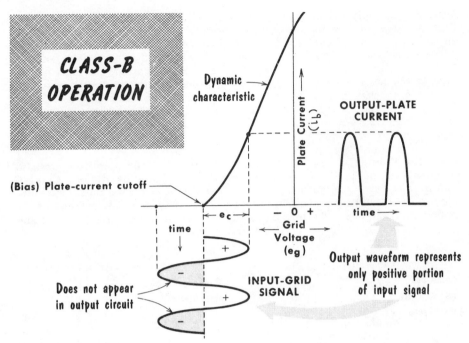

In a Class-B amplifier, plate current flows during 180° of the input grid volt-age cycle. That is, a Class-B amplifier is biased at cutoff, so that there is no plate current flow when no signal is applied. Plate current flows only during the positive half of the input signal. Since the output plate current waveform represents only the positive half of the input signal, this class of operation cannot be used where an exact replica of the entire input must be reproduced in the output circuit. Single-ended (single-tube) Class-B ampli-fiers are used in radio-frequency amplifier stages having a parallel-tuned circuit as the plate load. This tank circuit provides the second half of the output cycle by means of L-C charge and discharge action. In audio ampli-fication, where the output waveform must be exactly like the input waveform for minimum distortion, two tubes must be used in "push-pull," an arrange-ment which we shall discuss later, where each tube supplies that half of the output waveform not supplied by the other.

Class-B amplifiers are characterized by medium power output, medium plate efficiency (approximately 50%), and moderate power amplification. Since the a-c component of plate current is proportional to the amplitude of the grid signal voltage, the output power is proportional to the square of this voltage. Being biased at plate current cutoff, the positive cycle must swing through the nonlinear portion of the dynamic characteristic, producing a cer-tain amount of distortion in the output. When used in high-power amplifiers, Class-B operation is often such that the positive cycle swings into the positive grid voltage area, and the grid draws current.

Class-AB and Class-C Operation

A Class-AB amplifier operates in the region between Class-A and Class-B. That is, plate current in a Class-AB amplifier flows for more than 180° of the input grid voltage cycle, but for less than 360°. In Class-AB$_1$ operation, a limit is set on the input signal swing, so that the grid is not driven positive during any part of the input cycle. In Class-AB$_2$ operation, the input signal exceeds the negative bias on the positive swing, and the grid goes positive, causing grid current to flow. Class-AB operation is essentially a compromise between the low distortion of the Class-A amplifier and the high efficiency of the Class-B amplifier. Single-tube Class-AB operation cannot be used in audio circuits.

The Class C amplifier is used primarily as an r-f power amplifier in radio transmitters, and is discussed in Volume 6. The characteristic of a Class-C amplifier is that plate current flows for less than 180° of the input grid voltage cycle. As a result, Class-C amplifiers are noted for their extreme efficiency, upward to 80%. The high distortion of a Class-C amplifier is overcome by the "flywheel" effect of tuned circuits.

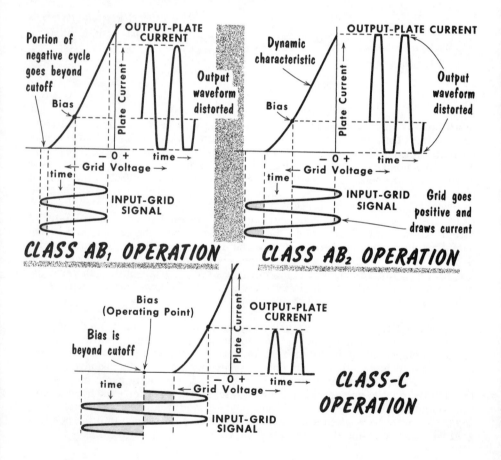

Fixed Bias and Self-Bias

In any amplifier, the location of the operating point on the dynamic characteristic curve (hence, the class of amplifier operation) depends on the d-c grid bias voltage. Basically, there are two types of bias – fixed bias and self-bias. Fixed bias is usually supplied from a separate voltage source, such as cells, or from a negative voltage tap in the power supply. The fixed bias is generally placed in series with the grid signal input. The d-c bias voltage is applied so that the grid is made negative with respect to the cath-

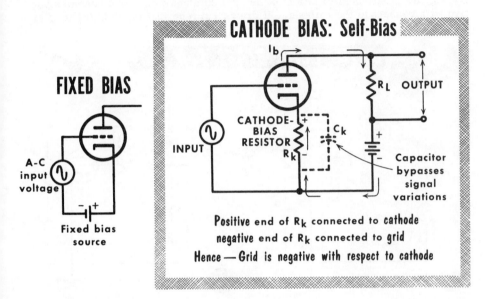

FIXED BIAS

A-C input voltage

Fixed bias source

CATHODE BIAS: Self-Bias

I_b

R_L OUTPUT

INPUT

CATHODE-BIAS RESISTOR R_k

C_k

Capacitor bypasses signal variations

Positive end of R_k connected to cathode
negative end of R_k connected to grid
Hence — Grid is negative with respect to cathode

ode. The total voltage between cathode and grid is thus equal to the sum of the d-c bias voltage plus the instantaneous value of the signal voltage. We should remember, however, that the d-c bias voltage is completely independent of the signal voltage.

The most common form of self-biasing is cathode bias. This is accomplished by placing a resistor (R_k) in series with the cathode circuit so that all plate and screen current must flow through it. The voltage drop across R_k is then such as to make the grid negative with respect to the cathode. With zero signal input, the current through R_k establishes the fixed grid bias. An applied input signal results in plate current variations, and hence, variations in the voltage drop across R_k. To prevent these variations and maintain a steady d-c bias, a bypass capacitor (C_k) is placed in parallel with R_k. Basically, this is a simple R-C filter. As the voltage drop across R_k reaches maximum, C_k charges to the full wave. When the voltage drop across C_k falls off, C_k discharges across R_k to maintain the zero signal value. The overall effect, as in the case of power supply filters, is to maintain a relatively constant voltage drop across R_k. In our study of amplifier circuits, we shall discuss values of R_k and C_k.

Grid-Leak Bias

Grid-leak bias is another form of self-bias. In circuit A, the value of C_g is sufficiently large so that at the input signal frequency, its capacitive reactance is small compared to the resistance of R_g, whose value is large. No bias voltage exists for zero signal voltage. When the a-c signal voltage is applied, it appears across R_g, making the grid alternately positive and negative with respect to the cathode.

During the positive alternation of the applied signal, the grid becomes positive with respect to the cathode. It draws current that flows in the grid cir-

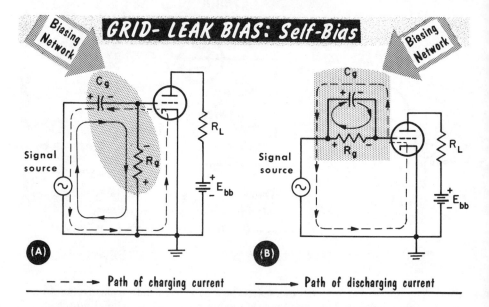

GRID- LEAK BIAS: Self-Bias

(A)   (B)

– – – ⟶ Path of charging current   ⟶ Path of discharging current

cuit, charging C_g to the maximum or peak value of the input voltage. The capacitor plate connected to the grid becomes negative. The charging current path is through the tube. During the negative alternation of the signal voltage, the grid becomes negative with respect to the cathode. C_g discharges slightly through resistor R_g, which has a high value. The top of R_g becomes negative with respect to the bottom. During the next cycle of the input voltage, C_g charges up again to full charge, then again slightly discharges, maintaining the voltage across R_g. Due to the action of $R_g C_g$, a d-c bias voltage is developed across R_g and applied to the grid of the tube.

Another means of obtaining grid-leak bias voltage is to connect C_g in parallel with R_g. The operation of circuit B is similar to the one described above, but the discharge current path of C_g is through R_g alone. The charging current paths are identical. The average voltage drop across R_g is the d-c grid bias voltage. The total grid voltage is the sum of the d-c bias voltage plus the input signal voltage. In both grid-leak bias voltage circuits, the value of the grid bias voltage depends on the signal voltage and the grid resistor.

Audio-Frequency Amplifiers

Now that we have discussed the basic amplifier circuit, we can begin the study of amplifier characteristics. A very common classification of amplifiers is audio-frequency (a-f) and radio-frequency (r-f) types. We shall take up first a-f amplifiers (sometimes called low-frequency amplifiers). Basically they are designed to amplify electrical signals of from about 30 to 15,000 hertz. These are called audio-frequencies because air moving back and forth at that rate can be "heard" by the human ear. While the range of hearing varies from person to person, 30 to 15,000 hertz represents an average hearing range. Certain animals, notably bats, have a hearing range that extends well beyond 15,000 hertz.

Two principal types of a-f amplifiers are voltage and power. Primarily, a voltage amplifier is designed to produce a large output voltage with respect to the input voltage. A power amplifier develops primarily a large signal current in the output circuit. Schematically, there is no way of distinguishing between voltage and power amplifiers except by their types of loads, a power amplifier in a radio receiver generally being used to drive a loudspeaker. In most instances, one stage of audio amplification is insufficient to accomplish most needs. Audio amplifiers must be cascaded; that is, the output of one feeds into the input of a second. The arrangement of transferring electrical energy from one stage to another is called coupling, and as we shall see, the type of coupling used greatly affects the amplifier frequency characteristics.

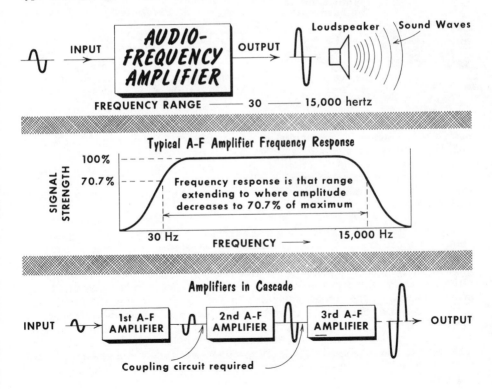

Amplifier Distortion

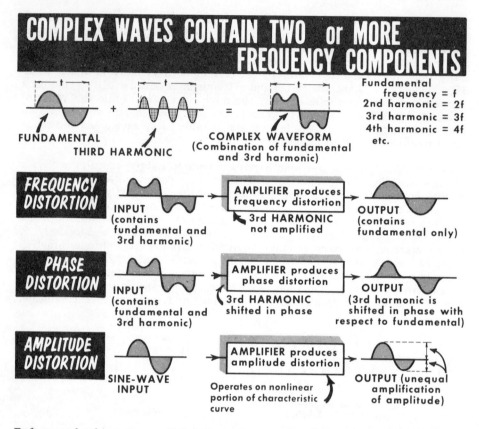

COMPLEX WAVES CONTAIN TWO or MORE FREQUENCY COMPONENTS

FUNDAMENTAL + THIRD HARMONIC = COMPLEX WAVEFORM (Combination of fundamental and 3rd harmonic)

Fundamental
frequency = f
2nd harmonic = 2f
3rd harmonic = 3f
4th harmonic = 4f
etc.

FREQUENCY DISTORTION
INPUT (contains fundamental and 3rd harmonic) → AMPLIFIER produces frequency distortion — 3rd HARMONIC not amplified → OUTPUT (contains fundamental only)

PHASE DISTORTION
INPUT (contains fundamental and 3rd harmonic) → AMPLIFIER produces phase distortion — 3rd HARMONIC shifted in phase → OUTPUT (3rd harmonic is shifted in phase with respect to fundamental)

AMPLITUDE DISTORTION
SINE-WAVE INPUT → AMPLIFIER produces amplitude distortion — Operates on nonlinear portion of characteristic curve → OUTPUT (unequal amplification of amplitude)

Before embarking on our study of coupling, let us give further thought to the nature of the signal being amplified. Regardless of whether the input signal voltage consists of a single sine waveform or a complex wave containing many frequencies, the function of an amplifier is to strengthen the signal without introducing any distortion in the process. Three types of distortion that may occur in amplifiers are: frequency, phase, and amplitude or nonlinear distortion.

Frequency distortion occurs when some frequency components of a signal are amplified more than others. For example, a signal consisting of a fundamental and a third harmonic may pass through a two-stage amplifier which introduces frequency distortion by which only the fundamental has been amplified, and the third harmonic component does not appear in the output. In phase distortion, the output waveform is considerably different from the input because the phase of the third harmonic has been shifted with respect to the fundamental. If a signal is passed through a vacuum tube operating on any nonlinear part of its characteristic, amplitude distortion occurs. In this region, any change in grid voltage does not result in a change in plate current, which is directly proportional to the change in grid voltage.

The Decibel

Various voltage, current, and power gains and losses in electronic equipment are often spoken of in terms of <u>decibels.</u> This is an outgrowth from the telephone field, where the decibel was used as a mathematical expression that represented the property of the human ear to respond to <u>ratios</u> of sound intensity. Mathematically, the decibel is a logarithmic ratio, and is used in electronics as a shorthand notation for power ratios. The decibel is a <u>relative</u> unit of measurement that originally was used to express changes in audio power, and the ability of the human ear to recognize these changes. For instance, if an amplifier produced an output power through its loudspeaker of 10 watts, it would then have to increase its output power 10 times to 100 watts for our ear to detect twice as much "loudness" (2 is the logarithm of 100).

Mathematically, we define the decibel as being equal to $10 \times \log_{10}$ of $P2/P1$, where $P2$ is always the larger power in watts, and $P1$ is always the smaller power in watts. The expression "$\log_{10}$" merely describes the type of logarithms used, generally called <u>common</u> logarithms. Thus, it should be understood that the decibel is only a unit of comparing two levels; it does not give an absolute value for either. If we compare two voltages, we say that the decibel gain or loss is equal to $20 \times \log_{10}$ of $(E2/E1)$. This is because P has relationships of E^2/R and I^2R. Hence, currents would be written as $20 \times \log I2/I1$. This process is simplified by using the table below. For instance, let us assume that the output power of an amplifier is twice the input power. We look up the ratio of 2 in our table and find that it corresponds to 3 db. We then say the amplifier has a power gain of 3 db. The table is designed to read voltage, current, and power db projected from the ratio axis. When we have a loss, it is represented as -db.

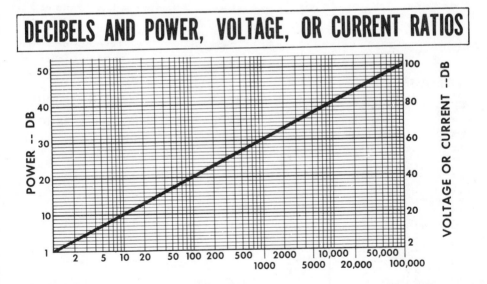

DECIBELS AND POWER, VOLTAGE, OR CURRENT RATIOS

RATIO

PRACTICAL EXAMPLES
ILLUSTRATING the USE of DECIBELS

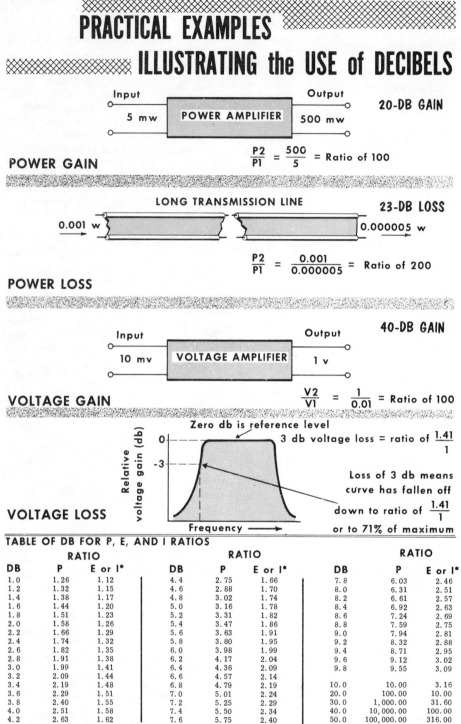

20-DB GAIN

Input — POWER AMPLIFIER — Output
5 mw → 500 mw

POWER GAIN

$$\frac{P2}{P1} = \frac{500}{5} = \text{Ratio of 100}$$

LONG TRANSMISSION LINE   **23-DB LOSS**

0.001 w →   → 0.000005 w

$$\frac{P2}{P1} = \frac{0.001}{0.000005} = \text{Ratio of 200}$$

POWER LOSS

40-DB GAIN

Input — VOLTAGE AMPLIFIER — Output
10 mv → 1 v

VOLTAGE GAIN

$$\frac{V2}{V1} = \frac{1}{0.01} = \text{Ratio of 100}$$

Zero db is reference level

Relative voltage gain (db)

3 db voltage loss = ratio of $\frac{1.41}{1}$

Loss of 3 db means curve has fallen off

VOLTAGE LOSS

down to ratio of $\frac{1.41}{1}$

or to 71% of maximum

Frequency →

TABLE OF DB FOR P, E, AND I RATIOS

DB	P	E or I*	DB	P	E or I*	DB	P	E or I*
1.0	1.26	1.12	4.4	2.75	1.66	7.8	6.03	2.46
1.2	1.32	1.15	4.6	2.88	1.70	8.0	6.31	2.51
1.4	1.38	1.17	4.8	3.02	1.74	8.2	6.61	2.57
1.6	1.44	1.20	5.0	3.16	1.78	8.4	6.92	2.63
1.8	1.51	1.23	5.2	3.31	1.82	8.6	7.24	2.69
2.0	1.58	1.26	5.4	3.47	1.86	8.8	7.59	2.75
2.2	1.66	1.29	5.6	3.63	1.91	9.0	7.94	2.81
2.4	1.74	1.32	5.8	3.80	1.95	9.2	8.32	2.88
2.6	1.82	1.35	6.0	3.98	1.99	9.4	8.71	2.95
2.8	1.91	1.38	6.2	4.17	2.04	9.6	9.12	3.02
3.0	1.99	1.41	6.4	4.36	2.09	9.8	9.55	3.09
3.2	2.09	1.44	6.6	4.57	2.14			
3.4	2.19	1.48	6.8	4.79	2.19	10.0	10.00	3.16
3.6	2.29	1.51	7.0	5.01	2.24	20.0	100.00	10.00
3.8	2.40	1.55	7.2	5.25	2.29	30.0	1,000.00	31.60
4.0	2.51	1.58	7.4	5.50	2.34	40.0	10,000.00	100.00
4.2	2.63	1.62	7.6	5.75	2.40	50.0	100,000.00	316.00

*May be used only when input and output impedances are equal.

Frequency Response

It is seldom that an amplifier is called upon to handle a single frequency. Much more often, it must handle a wide range of frequencies. Because of various factors, to be discussed later, most amplifiers have a characteristic of being able to amplify a certain middle range of frequencies relatively evenly, and then providing less amplification for both the lower and higher range of frequencies. If we draw a graph of this, using the vertical axis to represent relative gain, and the horizontal axis to represent frequency, we will get what is known as a frequency-response curve. It is really a "picture" of how an amplifier will amplify a wide range of frequencies. The vertical axis can be measured in terms of current, voltage, or power, or it could measure relative gain in terms of db.

The horizontal axis is usually logarithmically spaced rather than linearly spaced. That is, the distance from 10 hertz to 100 hertz is the same as the distance from 100 to 1000, or 1000 to 10,000. The reason for this type of scale is that the ratios of the frequency are important, and a very wide range of frequencies may thus be shown on the graph. When the logarithmic frequency scale is used, the frequency response for frequencies as low as 20 cycles can be shown, as well as for 20,000 hertz. This is not true of a linear frequency scale. Very often, the vertical axis is measured in terms of decibels, with the maximum amplification at the middle frequencies equal to 0 decibels. Thus, as the curve falls off at the high and low frequencies, the graph indicates how much db loss takes place at these frequencies.

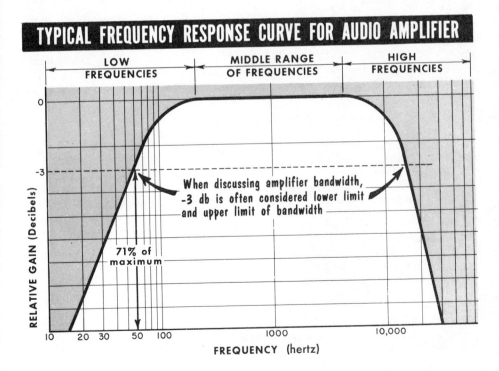

TYPICAL FREQUENCY RESPONSE CURVE FOR AUDIO AMPLIFIER

When discussing amplifier bandwidth, -3 db is often considered lower limit and upper limit of bandwidth

71% of maximum

The dynamic characteristics of a tube can be described as a graphic portrayal of tube behavior under load conditions.

When a signal source and a load are used, the following mathematical relationships hold true: $e_c = E_{cc} + e_g$; $e_b = E_{bb} - i_b R_L$; $e_{RL} = i_b R_L$.

A load line displays the way in which the output of the plate supply voltage is distributed between the load and the internal resistance of the tube under different conditions of plate current.

The dynamic transfer characteristic curve correlates the plate current — grid voltage relationship with the load present in the circuit.

The total change in plate voltage is always equal to the change in voltage across the load.

Nonlinearity in electron tubes is a source of distortion and is highly undesirable.

If an amplifier is to operate without grid current, the amount of fixed negative bias must be at least equal to the peak value of the positive half of the input grid signal.

The effect of interelectrode capacitance can lead to feedback and oscillation.

Gain is the ratio of output to input. The greater the number of stages in an amplifier, the greater the gain.

An a-f amplifier amplifies frequencies in the audio range.

The amount of distortion in an amplifier depends partially on the linearity of its dynamic characteristics. The more linear the characteristic, the less the distortion.

A Class-A amplifier is one in which plate current flows all the time. The input grid signal operates along the most linear portion of the dynamic characteristic.

Plate efficiency is the ratio of a-c power output developed across the load to the d-c power supplied to the plate.

Grid-leak bias is obtained through the action of the input grid signal.

In an electron tube circuit, the a-c grid voltage, plate current, and voltage drop across R_L are all in phase, and 180° out of phase with plate voltage.

REVIEW QUESTIONS

1. What is a dynamic transfer characteristic curve?
2. How would you go about drawing a load line for a given set of grid-family curves?
3. What does a load line indicate?
4. Why does nonlinearity of characteristic curves cause distortion? How can it be minimized?
5. Is interelectrode capacitance more noticeable at higher or lower frequencies? Why?
6. What is meant by the operating point of a tube?
7. How is cathode bias developed?
8. How is grid-leak bias developed?
9. In a triode amplifier, what is the phase relationship between grid voltage, plate current, and plate voltage?
10. Explain Class-A operation.
11. What is meant by an amplifier's frequency response?
12. Compare the plate efficiencies of Class-A, -AB, -B, and -C amplifiers.

Resistance-Capacitance Coupling

The most common type of coupling network for transferring electrical energy from one circuit to another, is the R-C, or resistance-capacitance type. This is generally known as resistance coupling. Our diagram shows two triode amplifiers coupled by an R-C coupling circuit. When a varying signal voltage e_g is applied to the grid of V1, it causes the plate current to vary through the tube and through R_L. The changing current through R_L produces a varying voltage drop across it. The output signal of V1 is the varying voltage between its plate and ground. This output voltage is equal to the fixed plate supply voltage minus the varying voltage across R_L. It is desirable to make R_L as large as possible. As this resistance is increased (within limits), a larger signal voltage appears across it. As a result, the output voltage from V1 is increased, and the stage is said to have greater amplification. There is a limit, however, to the value of R_L; if it is made too large, it produces an excessive d-c voltage drop. This reduces the plate voltage on the tube and the resultant plate current, so that the V1 output is reduced. Typical values for

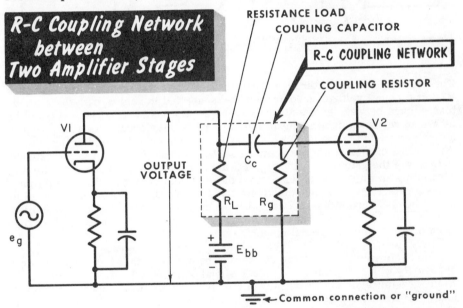

R-C Coupling Network between Two Amplifier Stages

RESISTANCE LOAD
COUPLING CAPACITOR

R-C COUPLING NETWORK

COUPLING RESISTOR

V1

OUTPUT VOLTAGE

C_c

R_L R_g

V2

e_g

+
E_{bb}
−

← Common connection or "ground"

R_L range from about 25,000 to 500,000 ohms, with the larger resistances used in pentode circuits where the internal plate resistance of the tube is very high, requiring a very high R_L for proper voltage gain.

The output signal of V1 is coupled through coupling capacitor C_c. This capacitor blocks the high positive plate voltage of V1 from being applied to the grid of V2. Because C_c blocks or prevents the passage of dc, it sometimes is referred to as a blocking capacitor. Since this capacitor must pass the varying signal voltage easily, its reactance should be low. Typical values of C_c range from 0.001 to approximately 0.1 µf. Larger values normally are not used because of their excessive stray capacitance to ground.

Resistance-Capacitance Coupling (Cont'd)

R-C COUPLED AMPLIFIER USING PENTODES

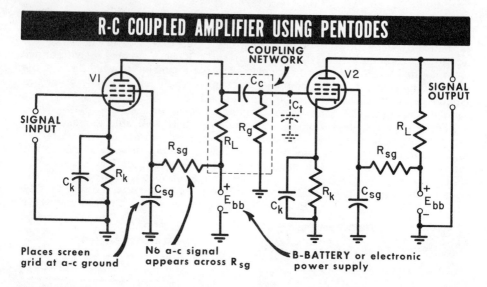

Places screen grid at a-c ground

No a-c signal appears across R_{sg}

B-BATTERY or electronic power supply

The a-c signal coupled through C_c is applied to grid resistor R_g of V2. The V2 input signal voltage drop across R_g is applied in series with the cathode bias voltage between grid and cathode of V2. R_g has other uses beside acting as a load across which the input signal to V2 is developed. R_g also provides a grid return for the grid of V2. That is, it connects the grid of the tube to this source of bias voltage – in this case, to one end of the cathode resistance. In this way the grid does not float. R_g also provides a discharge path for C_c, preventing an improper accumulation of electrical energy. Because R_g provides a path through which electrons can leak off C_c, it is often referred to as a grid-leak resistor. R_g can also be used as a source of grid-leak bias, and, as we shall learn, contact potential bias. Typical values for R_g range from 0.5 megohm to several megohms.

C_c and R_g form an a-c voltage divider. The output of this is the voltage drop across R_g which becomes the actual signal input to V2. Because of the infinite reactance of C_c to dc, all of the d-c voltage drop appears across it, and no dc from the plate of V1 is applied to the grid of V2. The reactance of C_c at audio frequencies is made much smaller than the resistance of R_g. Thus, very little of the a-c signal is lost across C_c and most all of it appears across R_g. C_t represents the total shunt capacitance of the circuit. It is a stray capacitance made up of the interelectrode capacitance of the tube, and wiring capacitances.

R-C coupling is also commonly used for pentode circuits, but screen grids of pentodes obtain their d-c operating voltages from series-dropping resistors R_{sg}. Capacitor C_{sg} bypasses any a-c signal voltage that appears in the screen-grid circuit, thereby preventing it from causing a fluctuation in screen-grid voltage. C_{sg} provides a virtual short-circuit for a-c signals from screen to ground.

Action in an R-C Circuit

To fully comprehend coupling action in R-C coupling, we must think of C_C and R_g as being in parallel with R_L, so far as a-c is concerned. While we see R_L in series with the plate supply voltage, in actual practice this supply would be bypassed by electrolytic filter capacitors in the power supply filter. So effectively, with respect to a-c, the low end of R_L is at ground potential. Thus any variation in voltage across R_L appears across C_C and R_g in series. From our illustration, we can see that coupling is nothing more than a continual charge and discharge action of C_C as it tries to maintain the voltage that is on the plate of the preceding stage. In so doing, an a-c voltage is

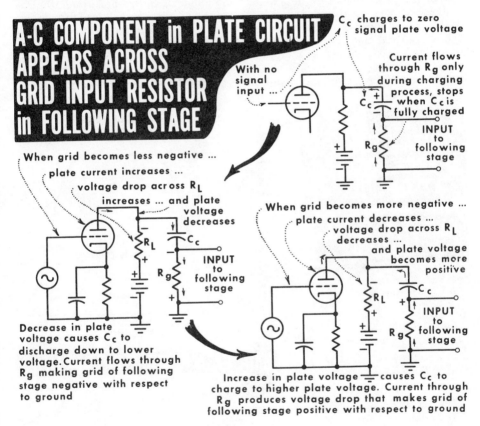

A-C COMPONENT in PLATE CIRCUIT APPEARS ACROSS GRID INPUT RESISTOR in FOLLOWING STAGE

C_C charges to zero signal plate voltage

With no signal input ...

Current flows through R_g only during charging process, stops when C_C is fully charged

C_C

R_g

INPUT to following stage

When grid becomes less negative ...
plate current increases ...
voltage drop across R_L increases ... and plate voltage decreases

R_L C_C

R_g

INPUT to following stage

Decrease in plate voltage causes C_C to discharge down to lower voltage. Current flows through R_g making grid of following stage negative with respect to ground

When grid becomes more negative ...
plate current decreases ...
voltage drop across R_L decreases ...
and plate voltage becomes more positive

R_L C_C

R_g

INPUT to following stage

Increase in plate voltage causes C_C to charge to higher plate voltage. Current through R_g produces voltage drop that makes grid of following stage positive with respect to ground

developed across R_g which becomes the input voltage to the following stage. In a-f amplifiers, the capacitance of C_C must be made sufficiently large so that its reactance will be extremely low when compared to the resistance of R_g. We want an a-c voltage drop only across R_g; this is useful. A voltage drop across the reactance of C_C is wasted. Hence, the reactance of C_C at the lowest audio frequency to be passed should be less than 10% of the value of R_g. As can be seen, the capacitance of C_C becomes a low-frequency limitation of a resistance-coupled amplifier.

Gain of R-C Coupled Amplifier

The gain of an amplifier, or its ability to amplify a signal, is generally greater at one frequency than another. By plotting the gain of an amplifier at various frequencies, we obtain a frequency response curve or response characteristic which indicates the gain of an amplifier over a wide range of frequencies. Frequency is plotted along the horizontal or X axis, while relative voltage gain is plotted along the vertical or Y axis. As we see, the response of an R-C coupled a-f amplifier is flat over the middle range of frequencies and then falls off at either end. The low-frequency tapering is caused by the increase in reactance of C_c. As the frequency to be amplified gets lower and lower, the reactance of C_c gets higher and higher. In the meantime, the resistance of R_g remains constant. Therefore, a greater and greater portion of the output signal is being dropped across the capacitive reactance of C_c and less signal appears across R_g, which represents the input source of the following stage. At the high-frequency end, the interelectrode and wiring capacitances begin to take on a shunting effect, and more and more of the output voltage is bypassed to ground; hence, amplifier gain decreases.

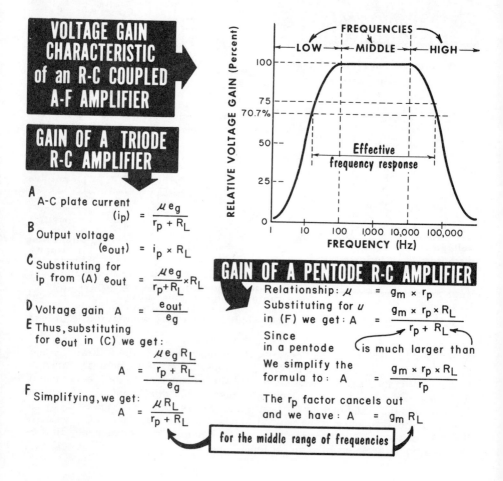

VOLTAGE GAIN CHARACTERISTIC of an R-C COUPLED A-F AMPLIFIER

GAIN OF A TRIODE R-C AMPLIFIER

A A-C plate current
$$i_p = \frac{\mu e_g}{r_p + R_L}$$

B Output voltage
$$e_{out} = i_p \times R_L$$

C Substituting for i_p from (A)
$$e_{out} = \frac{\mu e_g}{r_p + R_L} \times R_L$$

D Voltage gain
$$A = \frac{e_{out}}{e_g}$$

E Thus, substituting for e_{out} in (C) we get:
$$A = \frac{\frac{\mu e_g R_L}{r_p + R_L}}{e_g}$$

F Simplifying, we get:
$$A = \frac{\mu R_L}{r_p + R_L}$$

GAIN OF A PENTODE R-C AMPLIFIER

Relationship: $\mu = g_m \times r_p$

Substituting for μ in (F) we get:
$$A = \frac{g_m \times r_p \times R_L}{r_p + R_L}$$

Since in a pentode r_p is much larger than R_L

We simplify the formula to:
$$A = \frac{g_m \times r_p \times R_L}{r_p}$$

The r_p factor cancels out and we have:
$$A = g_m R_L$$

for the middle range of frequencies

Impedance Coupling

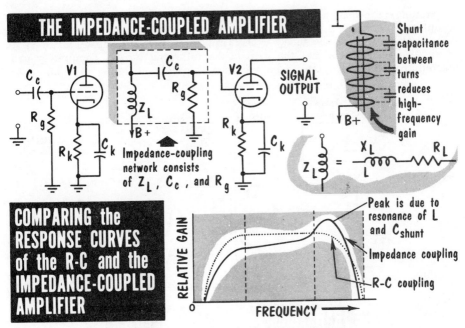

In the impedance-coupled amplifier, the plate load is an inductor; hence, instead of having a resistive load, we have an inductive load. Since all coils contain a certain amount of resistance, we refer to the load as an impedance, Z_L. To obtain as much amplification as possible, particularly at the lower frequencies, the inductance is made as large as is practical. A closed-shell type of inductor is generally used to avoid undesirable magnetic coupling. Because of the low resistance of an inductive load, the d-c voltage drop across it is small, and a greater amount of the supply voltage is available at the plate of the tube. The important characteristic of an inductive load is that its impedance changes with frequency. At low frequencies, its reactance is low; as the input frequency increases, the reactance (and hence, impedance) increases. As a result, impedance coupling is generally used in amplifiers where a relatively narrow range of frequencies are to be amplified.

The gain of the impedance-coupled amplifier is the ratio of the signal voltage drop developed across Z_L to the input signal voltage. Hence, the low-frequency limitation of this type of coupling is in the decreasing reactance of Z_L and the increasing reactance of C_c. At the higher frequencies, the shunt capacitance between the turns of the inductor reduces the gain, as well as the shunt capacitance of the circuit itself. In some situations, shunt capacitance may be sufficient to resonate with the inductance to cause a high peak to occur in the frequency response curve. The outstanding feature of this type of amplifier is that almost all of the plate supply voltage appears on the plate with very little wasted as a voltage drop across the load impedance. The cost of an inductor places this type of coupling at a disadvantage to R-C coupling.

Transformer Coupling

A transformer-coupled stage has certain advantages over other types of coupling. For one thing, the voltage amplification of this stage may exceed the amplification of the tube, if the transformer has a step-up turns ratio. Another advantage is that the grid of the following tube is completely protected from the d-c plate supply voltage through the isolated primary and

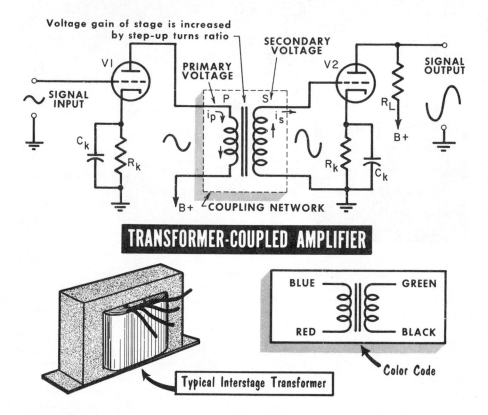

TRANSFORMER-COUPLED AMPLIFIER

Typical Interstage Transformer

Color Code

secondary windings.   Transformer coupling provides much of the frequency characteristics of impedance coupling in that the primary is an inductor. The frequency response curve would show that a transformer-coupled voltage amplifier has a relatively high gain and uniform frequency response over the middle range of frequencies, but poor response at both the low and high audio frequencies.   The low- and high-frequency limitations are much the same as those encountered in the impedance-coupled amplifier. Transformer coupling has the additional disadvantages of greater cost, greater space requirements, and the necessity for greater shielding.   Transformer coupling is seldom used in voltage amplifiers because its frequency response is poor compared to the R-C coupled amplifier. The additional voltage gain available by a step-up turns ratio is generally not sufficient compensation for its poorer frequency response.

Direct Coupling

In the coupling circuits we have studied so far, the coupling device isolates the d-c voltage of the plate circuit from the d-c voltage of the grid circuit, allowing only a-c components of the output to pass through the coupling device. In the direct-coupled amplifier, the plate of one tube is connected directly to the grid of the next tube without any intervening capacitor, transformer, or other coupling device. Since the plate of the first tube must have a positive voltage with respect to its cathode, and the grid of the next tube must have a negative voltage with respect to its cathode, proper circuit operation demands the use of a special voltage divider. This is obtained by using a multitap bleeder resistor across the output of the power supply.

This type of circuit is particularly effective with low-frequency amplification because the impedance of the coupling element does not vary with frequency. Thus, a direct-coupled amplifier is capable of amplifying very low variations of signal input voltage. Note that the plate load resistor of the first stage acts as the grid resistor for the following stage. When the tube voltages are properly adjusted to give Class-A operation, the circuit serves as a distortionless amplifier whose response is uniform over a wide frequency range. The particular disadvantage of the direct-coupled amplifier is in the severe demands made on the power supply to ensure voltage stability. Any change in the various voltages produces drift   This is especially troublesome in high-gain amplifiers, since drift that takes place in the input stage is then amplified before appearing in the output circuit.

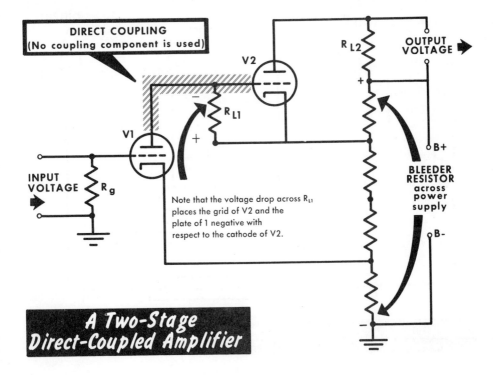

The Grounded-Grid Amplifier

All amplifiers discussed so far have made use of a common or grounded cathode; that is, the input signal is delivered into the grid cathode circuit with the output taken from the plate cathode circuit. Very often used at higher frequencies is the grounded-grid amplifier. In this circuit, the input voltage is applied to the cathode with the grid being grounded, and the output is taken from the plate and is in phase with the input signal. If the input voltage is applied between cathode and grid, it is the same as placing an opposite voltage between grid and cathode. (Making the grid 5 volts negative with respect to the cathode is the same as making the cathode 5 volts positive with respect to the grid.) No current flows in the grid circuit because it is negative with respect to the cathode and repels all electron flow. Current flows in the cathode circuit and it is the same current as flows in the plate circuit. In the grounded-cathode arrangement, there is no current in the input circuit; hence, the a-c input resistance is extremely high. In the grounded-grid amplifier, there is current flow, and the input resistance is quite low, for example, 2000 ohms. The control grid acts as a grounded shield between the output circuit, plate to ground, and the input circuit, cathode to ground; thus, electrical energy transfer is largely avoided between the input and output circuits through the capacitances of the tube. In the grounded-grid amplifier, the input voltage is 180° out of phase with the plate current, and is thus in phase with the output or plate voltage signal which appears across the plate load resistor.

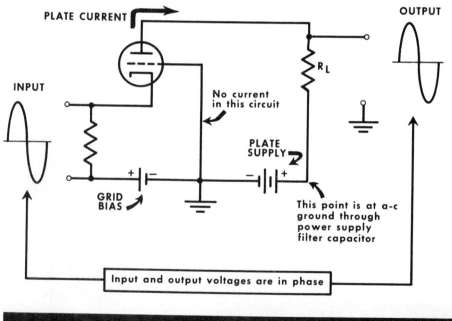

The GROUNDED-GRID AMPLIFIER

The Cathode Follower

CATHODE FOLLOWER (GROUNDED-PLATE) CIRCUIT
Provides no voltage gain

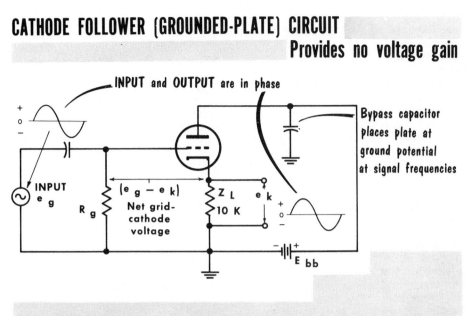

The cathode follower is essentially a grounded-plate amplifier in which the load impedance is located in the cathode circuit and the plate is at a-c ground through a bypass capacitor. The cathode follower is generally operated as a Class-A amplifier, the output of which appears across the unbypassed cathode resistor. This introduces degeneration (discussed later) and prevents the circuit from producing a voltage gain. The grid circuit, in drawing no grid current, presents a high input impedance. The load impedance, which may be anywhere from 50 to 20,000 ohms, presents a low output impedance. This circuit then becomes ideal for matching a high-impedance source to a low-impedance load.

The advantages obtained by the use of a cathode follower exist only at the price of a voltage gain which is less than unity or 1. However, a power gain is possible. The name cathode follower is derived from the output voltage which follows the input voltage; that is, the output voltage not only has the same waveform, but also the same instantaneous polarity (phase). Note that the amplifier output voltage e_k developed across Z_L is in series with the cathode and grid, and thus has a polarity that opposes the input signal e_g. Thus, the net grid-cathode voltage is $e_g - e_k$. Hence, the voltage e_k developed across the load impedance will always be somewhat less than the signal voltage e_g. However, voltage e_g can be developed across a high impedance, whereas E_k exists across a relatively small load impedance. In this way, the cathode follower acts as an impedance transformer in which power amplification can be obtained at the same time as the impedance level is reduced. The cathode follower has excellent response, especially at higher frequencies.

Decoupling and Bypassing

When amplifier stages are cascaded (that is, the output of one stage is fed into the input of the next stage), precautions have to be taken in circuits that are common to both stages. If the signals from one stage are not isolated from the signals of a previous stage, electrical energy may be fed back in such phase as to oppose the amplification of a signal. This undesirable feedback can be eliminated by isolating one stage from another in those areas where feedback can take place easily. The most common location for feedback problems is in the B+ lines - those lines feeding the screen grids and plates. Here, the signals from the various circuits are fed into the common power supply together with the d-c components. If signals from two successive stages produce voltage drops 180° out of phase across the common power supply impedance, undesirable feedback is produced. This can be eliminated by the use of decoupling networks.

The most common form is a simple R-C filter circuit in series with the plate load of a stage, in which the a-c component is bypassed to ground. To be effective, the reactance of the decoupling capacitor should be no more than 10% of the decoupling resistance at the lowest frequency to be handled by that circuit. Should the reactance of the decoupling capacitor become too great, a significant portion of the a-c component would take the return path through the decoupling resistor and the power supply to ground, rather than through the capacitor. When this occurs, degeneration takes place across the power supply impedance. In some instances, energy may be fed back in phase to produce undesired oscillation.

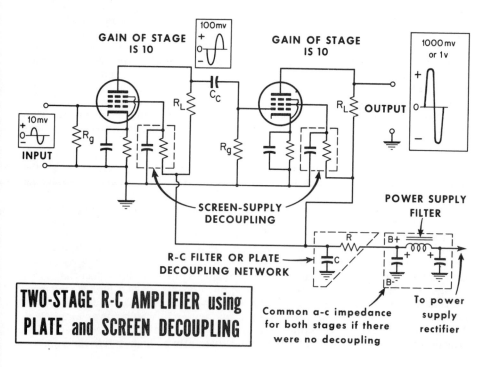

TWO-STAGE R-C AMPLIFIER using
PLATE and SCREEN DECOUPLING

Transformer-Type Phase Inverter

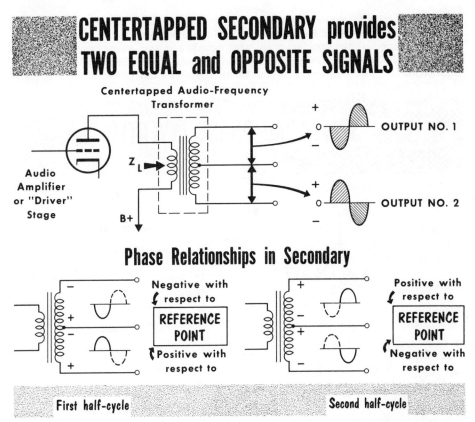

CENTERTAPPED SECONDARY provides TWO EQUAL and OPPOSITE SIGNALS

A very popular audio-frequency power amplifier is the push-pull type, which we shall discuss later. This circuit requires two input signals that are identical in every respect, except that one is 180° out of phase with the other. Various circuits are used to obtain these inputs. However, the simplest arrangement is through the use of an a-f interstage transformer in which the secondary is centertapped. The primary of this transformer, often called an input transformer, acts as the plate load impedance of the previous a-f voltage amplifier or "driver" stage. The secondary has more turns than the primary, and hence, provides a voltage step-up. The centertapped secondary assures that the voltages developed between the centertap and each end of the secondary are equal. Also, since the ends of the secondary are 180° out of phase, with the centertap as a reference point, the voltage developed between the centertap and the top half of the secondary will be 180° out of phase with the voltage developed between the centertap and the bottom half of the secondary. With the ends of the secondary connected to the two grids of the push-pull stage, the centertap must go to the negative side of the grid bias source; very often this is ground. The feature of this system is its simplicity. The secondary centertap provides two equal and opposite voltages.

The Split-Load Phase Inverter

One simple way to make a phase inverter is to connect one half of the plate
load resistance between B+ and plate, and the other half between cathode and
ground.   Since these resistances are equal and the same current flows
through both, each produces the same d-c voltage drop and the same audio
fluctuations.   For example, if the input signal to the phase inverter goes

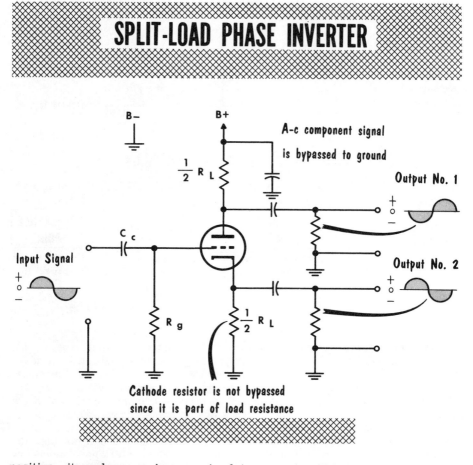

SPLIT-LOAD PHASE INVERTER

positive, it produces an increase in plate current.   This causes an increase
in voltage drop across the plate resistor, making the plate less positive with
respect to ground.   At the same time, this same plate current flowing through
the cathode resistor produces the same increase in voltage drop and makes
the cathode more positive with respect to ground.   Taking our two outputs
from the plate and cathode with respect to ground, we have equal and opposite
signals.   This circuit is simple, gives good balance, and provides good frequency response.   Its disadvantages are that it provides no amplification and
has a small signal-handling capacity.

The Paraphase Amplifier

Another phase-splitting arrangement is the so-called paraphase circuit. Basically, it uses two tubes. The output from the plate of one tube is fed by R-C coupling to one grid of the push-pull circuit. From this same point, a voltage-divider arrangement reduces the voltage and applies it to the grid of the second paraphase tube, which amplifies the voltage by as much as the resistance divider reduced it, producing an output voltage for driving the second push-pull grid. For instance, a positive fluctuation of 2 volts at the grid of the first paraphase tube may produce a negative fluctuation on its plate of, say, 20 volts. This 20 volts represents the output No. 1 of the paraphase amplifier. This 20-volt fluctuation is also divided to produce a negative fluctuation of 2 volts for the grid of the second paraphase tube which, in turn, becomes a positive fluctuation of 20 volts at the plate of the second tube. The positive 20-volt fluctuation represents output No. 2 from the circuit.

For this circuit to operate correctly, the voltage division produced by the resistor feeding the second paraphase tube must be in exactly the same ratio as the gain provided by the second paraphase tube. In the example given, the tube multiplies by 10 and the voltage divider divides by 10. This circuit has good handling capacity, gives some gain, and provides good frequency response. Its principal disadvantage is that the balance between the two outputs is sometimes difficult to maintain due to variations in circuit components.

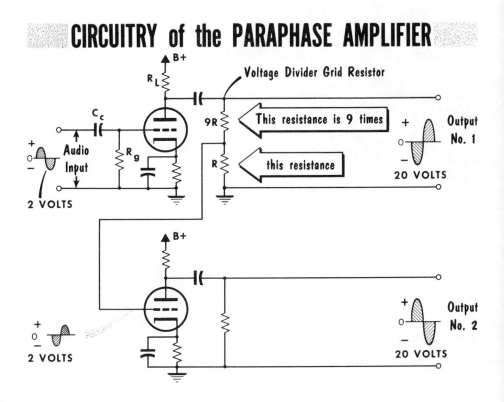

CIRCUITRY of the PARAPHASE AMPLIFIER

Power Amplifiers

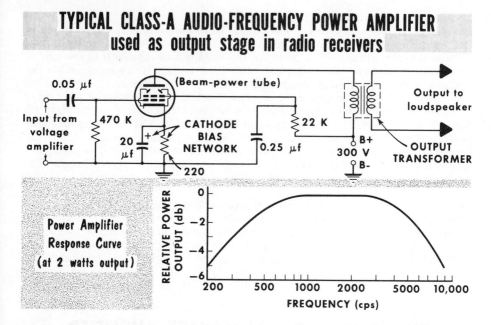

TYPICAL CLASS-A AUDIO-FREQUENCY POWER AMPLIFIER
used as output stage in radio receivers

0.05 μf

(Beam-power tube)

Output to loudspeaker

Input from voltage amplifier

470 K

20 μf

CATHODE BIAS NETWORK

22 K

0.25 μf

B+ 300 V

B-

OUTPUT TRANSFORMER

220

Power Amplifier Response Curve (at 2 watts output)

RELATIVE POWER OUTPUT (db)

FREQUENCY (cps)

The primary function of the voltage amplifiers just discussed is to increase the voltage of a signal to a higher value without distorting the waveform. Normally, voltage amplifiers consume no power from the preceding stage nor do they supply any appreciable power to the following stage; they merely provide voltage gain. The primary function of a power amplifier, however, is to deliver power to a load, any accompanying increase in signal voltage being of secondary importance. Output power is proportional to the square of the grid voltage. Hence, the power amplifier must usually be preceded by one or more stages of voltage amplification, to raise the signal to the proper value for operating or driving the power stage. In radio receivers, the power amplifier is used as the audio-output stage to drive a loudspeaker, which is considered the load. When used as a single tube in a-f amplification, the power amplifier must be Class-A operated.

Tubes used in audio power amplification are generally of the beam power type, capable of high power sensitivity and high plate current. The typical a-f power amplifier, used as the output stage of a receiver, looks much the same as a voltage amplifier, except that the plate load impedance is the primary of the output transformer. Conventional cathode bias is generally used. Many power output tubes used in radio receivers are capable of providing more than 5 watts output to the loudspeaker. Since the human ear is not particularly sensitive to distortion below about 5%, this much may be allowed in the output signal. The term "undistorted" output refers to distortion of less than 5%. Maximum undistorted power output is often achieved when the load impedance is approximately twice the plate resistance of the tube, and the plate current variations are at the maximum permissible value for Class-A operation.

Push-Pull Amplifiers

The next step in improving the power output capacity of an amplifier stage is
to use two tubes in a connection known as push-pull. This arrangement uses
transformer coupling, but there are two primaries (the primary winding has
two halves) through which the current flows in opposite directions. B+ is
connected to the center point of the primary, with the plate of one of the tubes
connected to each end.   The current therefore, flows from each plate outward through an equal number of turns to the center point.   This means that
the total magnetizing effect on the core of the transformer is neutralized as
far as the dc is concerned. (The transformer core only has to carry the
magnetization due to the audio fluctuation.) This simplifies the design and
cost of the transformer, but the big advantage is in the tube operation.

With a single tube, matching the output load to the tube plate resistance
results in a poor output waveform, which is rounded at the bottom and
sharpened at the top.   When the tubes are worked in push-pull, the current
flows in opposite directions around the transformer core, and consequently,
what is the top of the current waveform in the upper part of the winding, becomes the bottom of the current in the lower half of the winding.   Thus both
halves of the current waveform have a sharpened portion added to a rounded
portion, and the effect averages out, producing a much better waveform for
the load value used.   To achieve this, we must provide the correct audio
voltages at the grids of the tubes.   We shall consider this problem presently.

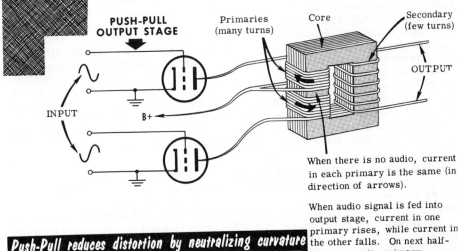

**PUSH-PULL
OUTPUT STAGE**

Primaries
(many turns)

Core

Secondary
(few turns)

OUTPUT

INPUT

B+

When there is no audio, current
in each primary is the same (in
direction of arrows).

When audio signal is fed into
output stage, current in one
primary rises, while current in
the other falls. On next half-
wave, opposite primary
currents rise and fall.

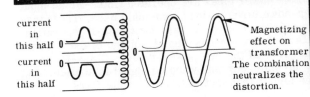

Push-Pull reduces distortion by neutralizing curvature

current
in
this half   0

current
in
this half   0

Magnetizing
effect on
transformer
The combination
neutralizes the
distortion.

The Practical Push-Pull Circuit

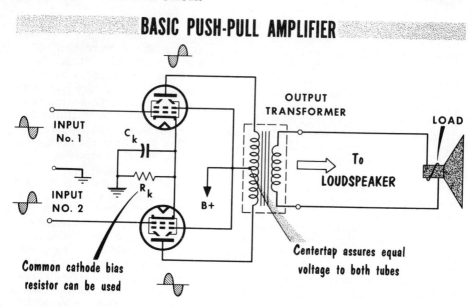

A number of advantages are to be gained by the use of a push-pull amplifier as the output stage of an a-f amplifier. Second harmonics, and all even-numbered harmonics, as well as even-order combinations of frequencies, will be effectively eliminated if the tubes are properly balanced, and if the frequencies are introduced within the output tubes themselves. Hum from the plate power supply, which may be present in the single-tube amplifier, is substantially reduced in the push-pull amplifier because ripple components in the two halves of the primary transformer are in phase, and tend to counter-act each other in the output. Plate current flow through the two halves of the primary winding is equal, and in opposite directions. Therefore, there is no d-c core saturation, and the low-frequency response is improved. Regenera-tion is also eliminated because signal currents do not flow through the plate voltage supply when the circuit is operated as a Class-A amplifier.

The last voltage amplifier preceding the push-pull power amplifier stage may be either resistance- or transformer-coupled to the power stage. If the power amplifier is operated Class-A or Class-AB, the driver commonly em-ploys resistance coupling because it affords a better frequency response. A phase-inverter tube, or section of a tube, must be used in connection with the resistance-coupled driver to provide the correct phase relation at the input of the push-pull stage. When the power tubes are operated Class-B, an input transformer employing a step-down turns ratio is commonly used. The trans-former not only supplies the grid current necessary for Class-B operation, but at the same time permits an instantaneous signal voltage of the correct polarity to be applied to the grids of the two power tubes. Class-B power amplifiers draw practically no plate current when no signal is applied, and their plate efficiency is much higher than that of Class-A amplifiers.

Triode Connection of Pentodes

Any pentode-type tube can be made to work as a triode-type tube. This is done by connecting the second grid directly to the plate, so that both swing together at the same voltage. Because the screen grid, in combination with the control grid, is principally responsible for controlling the plate current, the presence of the suppressor grid between the screen grid and plate does not materially alter the tube's performance from that of a triode.

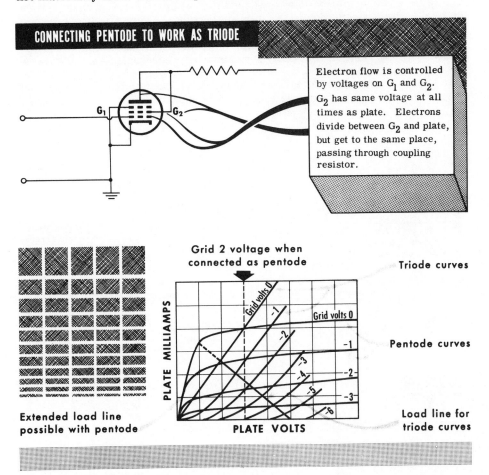

CONNECTING PENTODE TO WORK AS TRIODE

G_1 G_2

Electron flow is controlled by voltages on G_1 and G_2. G_2 has same voltage at all times as plate. Electrons divide between G_2 and plate, but get to the same place, passing through coupling resistor.

Grid 2 voltage when connected as pentode

Triode curves

PLATE MILLIAMPS

Grid volts 0

Grid volts 0

-1

-2

-3

-1

-2

-3

-4

-5

-6

Pentode curves

Extended load line possible with pentode

PLATE VOLTS

Load line for triode curves

With the best possible load resistance with triode-connected tubes, the voltage fluctuation between B+ and plate reaches little more than half the B+ supply voltage. Changing the method of connection to pentode alters the curve so that the zero grid voltage curve is pushed out into a "knee." This extends, very considerably, both the voltage and current fluctuation available in the plate circuit, which, in turn, triples or quadruples the power that any pair of tubes will give.

The Lowering of Distortion

Using two tubes in push-pull helps the waveform problems, so that the distortion produced by one tube cancels that of the other. This can be understood better if we think of each tube as having a <u>curved</u> load line. The input
voltages to the grids are equal but 180° out of phase. The plate voltages
likewise are out of phase because of the coupling between the two primary
windings of the output transformer. So the changes in plate current must adjust between the tubes to allow this condition, while the two of them supply
the <u>total</u> current fluctuation to the load at all points. The ratio between total
voltage and current fluctuations of both tubes is set by the load resistance
matched to the secondary of the transformer, but each tube feeds a load resistance whose value is constantly changing, as represented by the curves.

This effect can be extended further, to increase the efficiency of the output
stage. Normally the steady plate current is about half the maximum plate

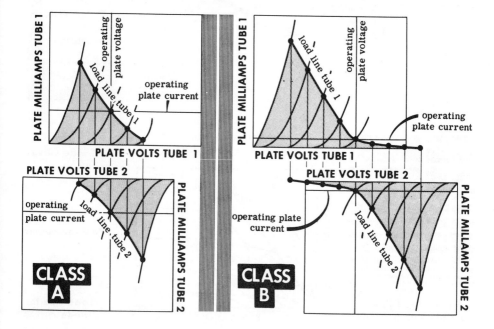

current (which occurs when the grid voltage fluctuation goes from the operating point up to zero). The current fluctuation in the tube at maximum
power level swings between almost zero current and twice the steady current. This sets a considerable limitation on the power-handling capacity of
the tube because the steady component is such a large proportion of the maximum current the tubes take. Using a greater negative bias on the grids of
the tubes makes the audio fluctuations carry the current from almost zero up
to a maximum in one direction, and cuts the tube off so that no current flows
in the other direction. This makes possible a considerable increase in
efficiency and available power output.

Power Output from a Class-A Stage

As an example, suppose that in ordinary push-pull (or Class-A with both tubes conducting current all the time), the operating point for each tube is 250 volts at 30 milliamperes, and that the load value presented to each tube is 5000 ohms with pentode operation. Disregarding the curves to make the calculation simpler (if approximate), the audio fluctuation should carry the plate between 100 volts at 60 milliamperes, and 400 volts at zero milliamperes.

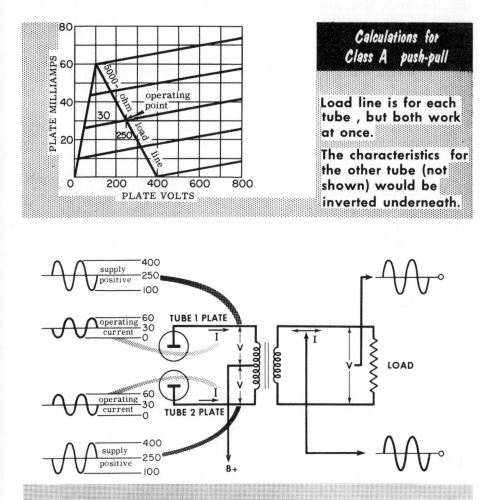

Calculations for Class A push-pull

Load line is for each tube, but both work at once.

The characteristics for the other tube (not shown) would be inverted underneath.

This represents a peak fluctuation from each tube of 150 volts and 30 ma in each direction, which is a peak power of (150 × 0.03) or 4.5 watts per tube, or 9 watts for the two tubes in push-pull. The average power, using a sine wave to drive the output, will be half this figure (4.5 watts for the two tubes).

Class-B Operation

If we wish to use an extreme economy measure, known as Class-B operation, we bias each tube for approximately zero current. (Actually it does not go quite to zero current because of the curvature of the characteristic, but it goes to where zero current would be if the tube characteristics were all straight. (This is called projected cutoff.) Using the same load line, the operating point for each tube would, theoretically, be 400 volts at zero milli-amperes. This means that the plate potential voltage will swing from 100 volts to 700 volts. Plate current will swing, during one half-cycle from zero to 60 milliamperes and back, while in the other half-cycle, no current flows in that tube.

The permissible maximum voltage on the plate is considerably increased by this method of operation (from 400 volts to 700 volts). There is less danger of breakdown between the plate and some other electrode when no plate cur-rent is flowing. There is, however, a maximum rated voltage even under this condition, which sometimes restricts the amount by which this method of operation can improve efficiency.

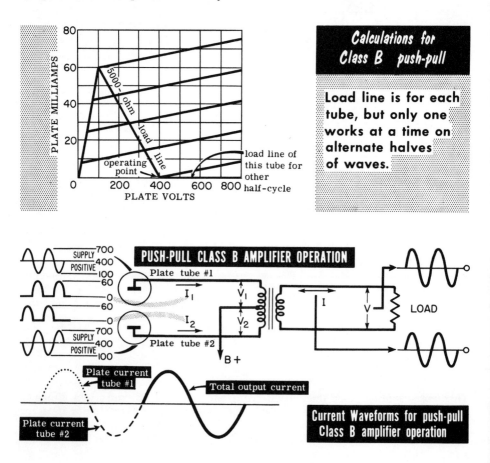

Calculations for Class B push-pull

Load line is for each tube, but only one works at a time on alternate halves of waves.

PUSH-PULL CLASS B AMPLIFIER OPERATION

Current Waveforms for push-pull Class B amplifier operation

Impedance Matching

OUTPUT TRANSFORMER PROVIDES CORRECT IMPEDANCE MATCH

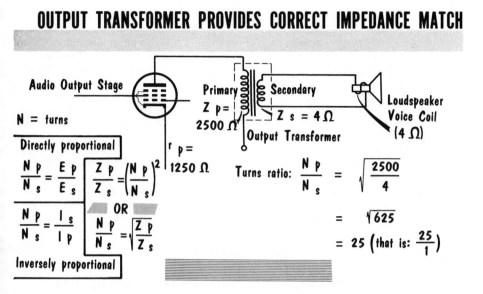

The output transformer used with a-f power amplifiers serves as an imped-ance-matching device. Since the plate resistance of a power amplifier tube may range from perhaps 1000 ohms to more than 20,000 ohms, and since the impedance of the loudspeaker may range down to 4 ohms, the output trans-former has a step-down turns ratio to provide the correct ratio of primary voltage and current to secondary voltage and current. The ratio of the two impedances that a transformer can match is equal to the turns ratio squared.

As a practical example, let us find the turns ratio needed for the transformer shown in our illustration. Since the plate resistance is 1250 ohms, the pri-mary impedance is considered as twice this value, to permit maximum un-distorted power output. The power fed to the 4-ohm voice coil, however, will be reduced unless the proper impedance is afforded by the transformer. The turns ratio between the primary and secondary that satisfies this con-dition is 25. The amount of power that can be handled by a transformer is determined by the current and voltage ratings of the windings. The primary frequency contains a d-c component that limits its inductance and frequency response. In a given transformer, the induced voltage is proportional to the frequency and the flux density. At low frequencies, the flux density is high and more distortion is introduced because of the saturation of the iron. The maximum allowable flux density is determined by the allowable distortion.

The output transformer causes a reduction in the output of a power amplifier at both the high and low frequencies. The reduced output at the low frequen-cies results from the shunting action of the transformer primary inductance on the load. The reduced output at the high frequencies results from the loss in voltage from the leakage reactances as a result of load current and capaci-tive current due to shunting capacitance.

The Output Transformer

The most common form of audio-frequency transformer is used in the output of an a-f power amplifier to match the circuit load impedance (usually a loudspeaker) to that required by the output tubes. The transformer here serves the additional purpose of avoiding both supply and audio losses, because the winding resistances are low compared to their respective impedances. The way impedance <u>reflects</u> in a push-pull transformer depends to some extent on the way tubes are operated. In Class-A, both tubes are delivering part of the power throughout the cycle, so the load is shared between them. If the ratio makes 16 ohms actual impedance equivalent to 6400 ohms at the primary, each tube has a load of 3200 ohms average. But in Class-B, only one half of the primary works at a time. The other is inactive for that half-cycle because its tube is cut off. The impedance transformation is based on the ratio to each half winding. If the whole ratio is 20:1, this is 10:1 each half. So 16 ohms connected to the secondary makes a load of 1600 ohms for each tube, but the tube takes the load for only half a cycle. A further advantage of push-pull operation in the transformer is that the magnet-

OUTPUT TRANSFORMER

MATCHES HIGH-IMPEDANCE VACUUM TUBE OUTPUT TO LOW-IMPEDANCE LOAD

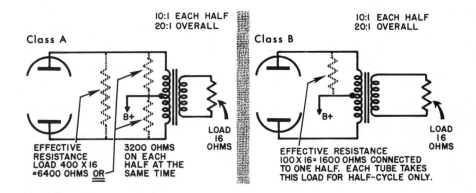

izing effect due to steady plate current cancels, whether the tubes are operated Class-A or Class-B. In turn, this allows a much smaller core to be used for providing an adequate primary inductance with the available turns in the primary winding.

The load reflects an impedance back into the primary. When current flows through the secondary winding, the resultant magnetic flux opposes the current in the primary winding and causes a new "impedance" to appear that was not present before secondary current began to flow. The effect of this inductive opposition is equivalent to adding an impedance in series with the primary winding. This impedance is known as <u>reflected</u> impedance. The reflected impedance becomes greater as the coefficient of coupling increases.

Negative and Positive Feedback

As the term implies, feedback involves the transfer of electrical energy from
the output of an amplifier back to its input. If the signal is fed back in phase
with the input signal, it is called positive or regenerative, because it adds to
the input voltage. If the signal fed back to the input is 180° out of phase with
the input signal, it is called negative, inverse, or degenerative, because it

Negative Feedback Reduces Amplifier Distortion

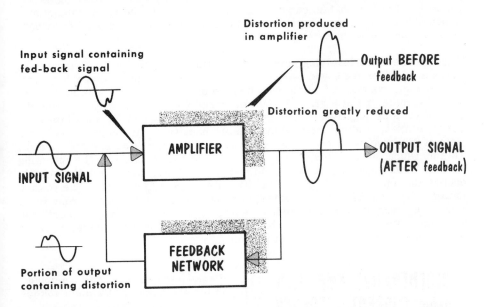

subtracts from the input voltage. In general, positive feedback is avoided in
amplifiers since it produces oscillation; negative feedback is used for the reduction of signal distortion. Negative feedback may be used to reduce nonlinear distortion – that is, to make the output waveform more nearly similar
to the input waveform by reducing nonlinearities that are introduced within
the amplifier tube itself.

The input signal applied to the grid of an electron-tube is amplified by an
amount determined by the μ of the tube, but any nonlinearities introduced
within the tube are not amplified. If a portion of the output is fed back 180°
out of phase with the input, the distortion component of this feedback signal
will be amplified along with the input signal. The amplified distortion component will tend to cancel the distortion component introduced within the tube,
and the output may be practically free of nonlinear distortion. It is necessary that the distortion occur in the plate circuit of the stage across which
negative feedback is to be applied, to separate the distortion from the desired
signal. However, the overall gain of the desired signal will also be reduced.
This reduction may be compensated for by increasing the number of stages.

Feedback Circuits

A popular method of obtaining feedback is shown in (A). This method employs current feedback. The cathode bypass capacitor has been omitted, producing degenerative action. When an input signal makes the grid less negative, plate current increases as does the voltage drop across R_k. Since R_k is not bypassed, the plate circuit signal currents flowing through R_k add to the bias produced by the zero-signal component. The grid-to-cathode voltage on the positive-going half-cycle is thus equal to the difference in the input and the drop across R_k. Hence, the net grid cathode voltage is not as great as it would be without feedback, because the drop across R_k is increased. The fact that an output voltage in phase with the input voltage may be developed across an unbypassed cathode resistor has been used in cathode followers and phase inverters.

Negative feedback involving more than one stage may be used. Diagram (B) shows a negative-feedback two-stage amplifier employing voltage feedback. In this case, special attention must be paid to the phase relations in the circuit. Assume that at a given instant the input voltage is such as to make the grid of V1 less negative. Plate current then increases in V1 and plate voltage decreases, making the grid of V2 more negative. At the same time, the plate of V2 becomes more positive because of the reduction in plate current. This increase in V2 plate voltage increases the charge of C1. The operating current flows through ground, up through R2 and R1, to the left plate of C1, making the top end of R2 more positive with respect to ground. The voltage increase across R2 acts in series with the input and the bias across R_k to reduce the magnitude of the positive-going signal on the grid. In short, the grid input signal is reduced by the amount of the feedback voltage, because these two voltages act 180° out of phase.

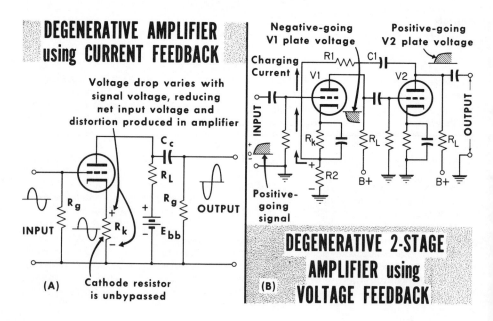

DEGENERATIVE AMPLIFIER using CURRENT FEEDBACK

Voltage drop varies with signal voltage, reducing net input voltage and distortion produced in amplifier

(A) Cathode resistor is unbypassed

Negative-going V1 plate voltage   Positive-going V2 plate voltage

DEGENERATIVE 2-STAGE AMPLIFIER using VOLTAGE FEEDBACK

(B)

The Loudspeaker

The conventional radio receiver may be considered as terminating in a loud-speaker. This is the device, often called a transducer, that converts electrical energy into mechanical energy, and finally, into acoustical energy. When the loudspeaker sets air in motion, the human ear should hear the same sounds that were emitted at the microphone of the transmitting station. The

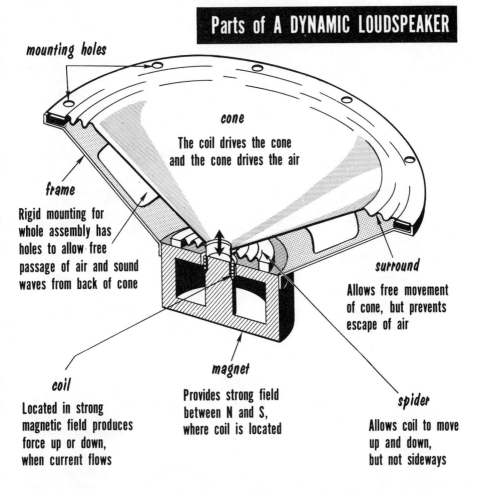

Parts of A DYNAMIC LOUDSPEAKER

mounting holes

cone
The coil drives the cone and the cone drives the air

frame
Rigid mounting for whole assembly has holes to allow free passage of air and sound waves from back of cone

surround
Allows free movement of cone, but prevents escape of air

coil
Located in strong magnetic field produces force up or down, when current flows

magnet
Provides strong field between N and S, where coil is located

spider
Allows coil to move up and down, but not sideways

diagram shows a cross-sectional view of the conventional loudspeaker in use today, the dynamic or moving-coil speaker. The voice coil impedance is usually about 4 ohms, although 8-ohm and 16-ohm voice coils are not uncommon. The voice coil is small and light and is suspended by a light flexible material that allows free movement at all frequencies. The requirements for getting maximum force to drive the cone (or diaphragm) are a strong magnetic field and as great a length of wire as is possible in the field.

The Loudspeaker Circuit

In the permanent magnet dynamic type of loudspeaker, a strong field is established between the pole pieces by a powerful permanent magnet. The flux is concentrated in the air gap between a permeable soft-iron core and an external yoke. The voice coil is mounted in the air gap. When a-c signal currents flow in the coil, a force proportional to the strength of the current is applied to the coil, and the coil is moved axially in accordance with the a-c signal. The loudspeaker diaphragm is attached to the voice coil and moves in accordance with the signal currents, thus setting up sound waves in the air. The corrugated diaphragm to which the speaker cone is attached keeps

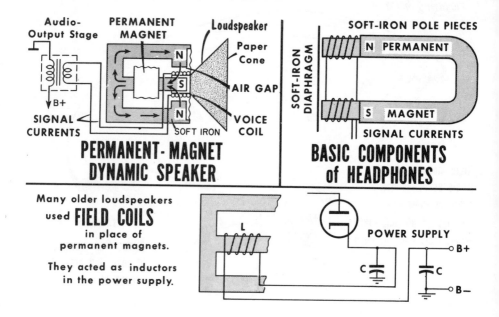

the cone in place and properly centered. An electromagnet may be used in place of the permanent magnet to form an electromagnetic dynamic speaker. However, in this instance sufficient d-c power must be available to energize the field.

Using the relatively sensitive headphone, signals can be heard directly from the output of the audio voltage amplifier. When no signal currents are present, the permanent magnet exerts a steady pull on the soft-iron diaphragm. Signal current flowing through the coils mounted on the soft-iron pole pieces develops a magnetomotive force that either adds to or subtracts from the field of the permanent magnet. The diaphragm thus moves in or out according to the resultant field. Sound waves then are reproduced that have amplitude and frequency (within the capability of the headphone) similar to the amplitude and frequency of the signal currents.

The Carbon Microphone

The CARBON MICROPHONE
produces a "PULSATING" DIRECT CURRENT

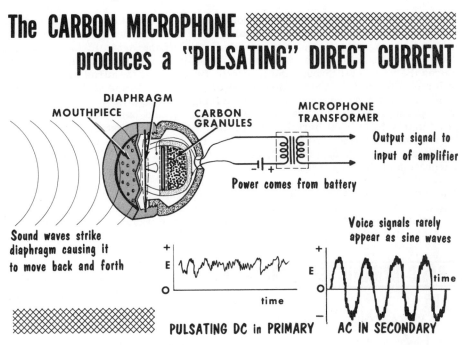

Although the microphone is not primarily associated with radio receivers, it is helpful to consider the microphone in conjunction with the loudspeaker in that the microphone is often the origin of electrical signals, and the loudspeaker the conclusion. The microphone is also a transducer. It converts acoustical or mechanical energy into electrical energy. There are many types of microphones, but here we shall consider the three most common — the carbon, dynamic, and crystal types. We shall compare them in terms of frequency response, impedance, and sensitivity.

The carbon microphone is the most common. It operates on the principle that a change in sound pressure on a diaphragm coupled to a small volume of carbon granules will cause a corresponding change in the electrical resistance of the granules. In the carbon microphone a diaphragm is mounted against carbon granules contained in a cup. To produce an output voltage, the microphone is connected in a series circuit which contains a battery and the primary of a microphone transformer. The pressure of the sound waves on the diaphragm coupled to the carbon granules causes the resistance of the granules to vary. Thus, a varying or pulsating direct-current in the primary produces an alternating voltage in the secondary of the transformer. This voltage has essentially the same waveform as that of the sound waves striking the diaphragm. Commercial types of carbon microphones give good response from 60 to 6000 hertz, and have a relatively high output. Their low internal impedance requires the use of a transformer. The main disadvantages are the requirement of an external voltage source and a high degree of noise.

The Dynamic and Crystal Microphones

The dynamic or moving-coil microphone consists of a coil of wire attached to a diaphragm and is so constructed that the coil is suspended and free to move in a radial magnetic field. Note its similarity to the dynamic loudspeaker. Sound waves striking the diaphragm cause it to vibrate. This vibration moves the voice coil through the magnetic field so that the turns cut the lines of force in the field. This action generates a voltage in the coil that has the same waveform as the sound waves striking the diaphragm. The dynamic microphone requires no external voltage source and has good fidelity (approximately 20 to 9000 hertz). Its output, however, is extremely low as is its internal impedance (50 ohms or less). Its low impedance makes it desirable for connection to relatively long transmission lines without excessive attenuation of the high frequencies.

The crystal microphone utilizes the property of certain crystals such as quartz or Rochelle salts, known as the piezoelectric effect. The bending of the crystal resulting from the pressure of the sound waves produces a difference of potential across the faces of the crystal. This voltage is applied to

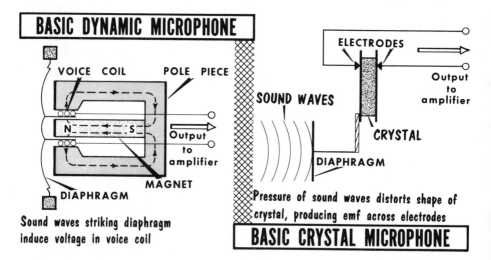

BASIC DYNAMIC MICROPHONE

VOICE COIL   POLE PIECE

N — — — — S   Output to amplifier

MAGNET

DIAPHRAGM

Sound waves striking diaphragm induce voltage in voice coil

ELECTRODES

Output to amplifier

SOUND WAVES

CRYSTAL

DIAPHRAGM

Pressure of sound waves distorts shape of crystal, producing emf across electrodes

BASIC CRYSTAL MICROPHONE

the input of an amplifier. The diaphragm may be cemented directly on one surface of the crystal or it may be cemented by mechanical coupling. A metal plate or electrode is attached to the other surface of the crystal. When sound waves strike the diaphragm, the vibrations of the diaphragm produce a varying pressure on the faces of the crystal, and therefore, a voltage is induced across the electrode. This voltage is essentially the same waveform as the sound wave striking the diaphragm. The crystal microphone has a relatively high output voltage as well as an extremely high impedance (several hundred thousand ohms). It is comparatively light, requires no battery, and has an excellent frequency response (up to 17,000 hertz). Its output is much higher than that of the dynamic microphone. It is widely used in that it can take rough handling while producing a high output voltage.

Radio-Frequency Amplification

Up to this point we have considered amplifiers designed primarily for the strengthening or amplification of a-f signals; that is, frequencies extending to about 16,000 hertz. In radio communications, receivers must also be able to handle frequencies well up into the megahertz range. For example, the standard radio broadcast band is from 535 kHz up to 1605 kHz. Above this there is the so-called "shortwave" bands which extend beyond 100 MHz (100,000,000

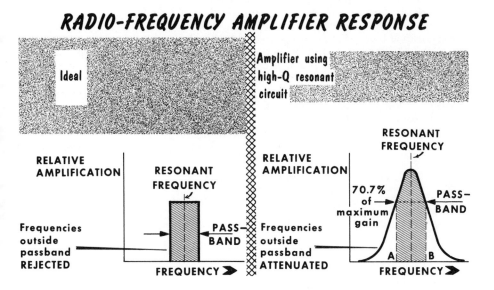

hertz). Amplification of these signal frequencies involve two basic changes: the tubes used are almost exclusively pentodes because of their low interelectrode capacitances (important at high frequencies) and methods of coupling. In general, r-f amplifiers utilize tuner or resonant circuits as grid loads, plate loads, or both.

An r-f amplifier is judged on effective gain at its tuned frequency, frequency response to signals lying at each side of the resonant frequency, and ability to discriminate against frequencies immediately adjacent to the passband. The band of frequencies to be passed by an r-f amplifier is generally a very small percentage of the resonant frequency. The tuned r-f circuits of a receiver operating at 1000 kHz must pass a band of 10 kHz—only 1%. An ideal r-f amplifier may be viewed as a bandpass filter having a response of that shown. Practical resonant circuits cannot be made to give this perfection. However, when the tuning components have a sufficiently high Q, this performance can be approached quite closely. The selectivity of a receiver is its ability to amplify a given band of desired frequencies and reject all others. The narrowest possible bandpass is not always desired. In some forms of communications, we purposely broaden the bandpass since the received signal covers a broad range; in others we make the response as narrow as possible. This will be covered in our discussion on receivers.

Tuned R-F Amplifiers

An important part of the coupling circuit of a tuned amplifier is the resonant circuit. This is used in plate circuits because it offers a high impedance at the desired frequency and a low impedance at other frequencies, thus permitting high amplification of a relatively narrow band of frequencies. In addition, the limitations imposed on untuned amplifiers by interelectrode and distributed capacitances are used to advantage because these capacitances become part of the tuned circuit. An r-f amplifier may be single- or double-tuned, depending on whether the plate circuit only, or both the plate and grid circuits, contain a tuned circuit. Our diagram shows the three common forms of tuned-amplifier circuits. In (A), the tuned circuit acts merely as a parallel L-C circuit, presenting a high plate impedance at resonance and a lower impedance above and below resonance. We can consider this circuit as being impedance-coupled. The single-tuned transformer-coupled amplifier of (B) is commonly used as a Class-A r-f voltage amplifier. Here magnetic coupling is used, with frequency selection taking place in the grid circuit of the second stage. Circuit (C) is double-tuned and transformer-coupled, with tuned circuits in the plate and grid circuits of coupled stages.

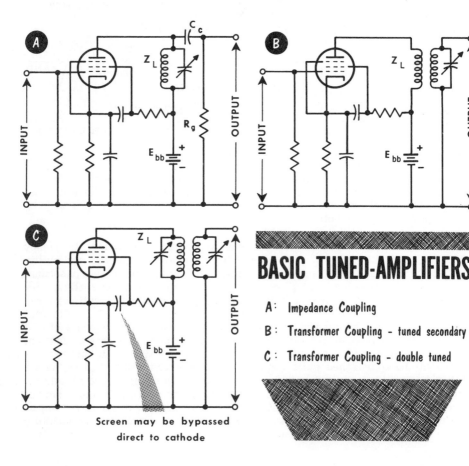

BASIC TUNED-AMPLIFIERS

A: Impedance Coupling

B: Transformer Coupling - tuned secondary

C: Transformer Coupling - double tuned

Screen may be bypassed direct to cathode

R-F Amplifier Coupling Characteristics

In tuning, the values of either L or C can be varied. C is varied by a variable capacitor; L can be varied by varying the powdered-iron core in the transformer. The powdered-iron core provides extremely high Q. Circuit Q is extremely important in that it determines the sharpness of the frequency response curve. A high-Q circuit gives a very sharp response, coupled with high gain, because of the extremely high impedance of the parallel resonant circuit. Using the double-tuned transformer, a relatively narrow band of frequencies may be amplified and frequencies outside this band are sharply reduced. These characteristics make this type of coupling highly desirable in intermediate amplifiers (which are discussed in Volume 4). The frequency bandpass is determined largely by the coupling between the primary and secondary of the r-f transformer. As can be seen from the curve, the degree of coupling may be varied to obtain a particular frequency response.

For low-power operation such as required in receivers, pentode r-f amplifiers, because of their low grid-to-plate capacitance, provide the highest gain with the least tendency to break into self-oscillation. Bypassing and decoupling become increasingly important at the higher frequencies. For maximum gain, pentode r-f amplifiers use high-Q circuits and tubes having a high mutual conductance.

DEGREE of COUPLING AFFECTS FREQUENCY RESPONSE

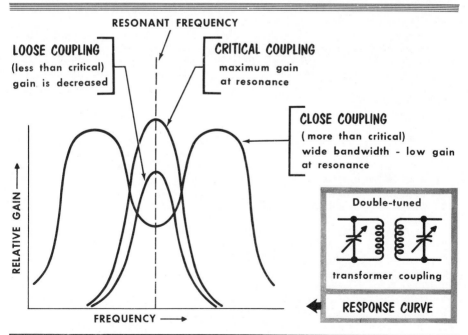

RESONANT FREQUENCY

LOOSE COUPLING
(less than critical)
gain is decreased

CRITICAL COUPLING
maximum gain
at resonance

CLOSE COUPLING
(more than critical)
wide bandwidth - low gain
at resonance

RELATIVE GAIN ⟶

FREQUENCY ⟶

Double-tuned

transformer coupling

RESPONSE CURVE

When the output of one stage is coupled to the input of another stage, a coupling network is used for transferring the energy.

One of the most common types of coupling networks is the R-C arrangement. The plate of one amplifier stage is connected to the grid of the following stage through a coupling capacitor. Resistors are used as the plate load and in the grid circuit.

A voltage gain or response characteristic curve indicates the amount of voltage gain an amplifier has over a wide range of frequencies.

The response characteristic of an R-C coupled amplifier drops off at the low frequencies because of the high reactance presented by the coupling capacitor.

The response characteristic of an R-C coupled amplifier drops off at the high frequencies because of the low reactance presented by the interelectrode, stray, and wiring capacitances.

In a transformer-coupled amplifier, the primary of the transformer is connected in the plate circuit of one tube and the secondary is connected in the grid circuit of the second tube.

If the feedback signal in an amplifier aids the original input signal, the feedback is called regenerative or positive. If the feedback signal opposes the original input signal, it is called degenerative, negative, or inverse.

A push-pull amplifier consists of two tubes arranged so that the plate current of one tube is 180° out of phase with the plate current of the other tube. The magnitudes of the currents are equal.

The input-grid signals for a push-pull amplifier are obtained from a transformer which has a centertapped secondary, or from a paraphase amplifier.

Compared to single-tube operation, less distortion is obtained in push-pull operation since its dynamic characteristic is more linear. Also, a greater grid-signal swing is permissible.

The dynamic loudspeaker operates on the basis of interacting magnetic fields from the voice-coil signals and the permanent magnet.

If the output waveform of an amplifier is identical with its input waveform, the amplifier is said to be distortionless. Types of distortion include amplitude distortion, frequency distortion, phase distortion, and harmonic distortion.

REVIEW QUESTIONS

1. What is the fundamental difference between voltage and power amplifiers?
2. What is the function of a coupling network?
3. What is the function of a d-c blocking capacitor?
4. Why does the voltage gain of an amplifier decrease at the low and high frequencies?
5. What are the advantages and disadvantages of transformer coupling?
6. Give an important application of the cathode follower.
7. What is a paraphase amplifier?
8. What advantages are realized from the push-pull amplifier?
9. What is the purpose of impedance matching?
10. Describe the operation of the dynamic loudspeaker.
11. Describe the operation of the carbon microphone.
12. Name some basic differences between r-f and a-f amplifiers.

Oscillation

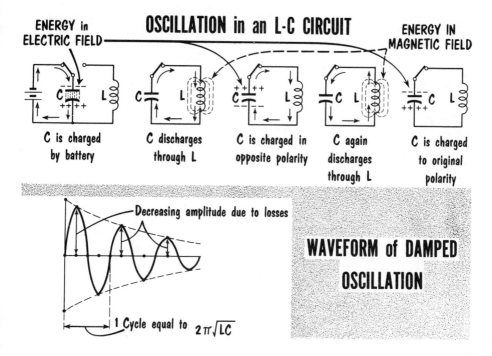

OSCILLATION in an L-C CIRCUIT

ENERGY in ELECTRIC FIELD

ENERGY IN MAGNETIC FIELD

C is charged by battery

C discharges through L

C is charged in opposite polarity

C again discharges through L

C is charged to original polarity

Decreasing amplitude due to losses

WAVEFORM of DAMPED OSCILLATION

1 Cycle equal to $2\pi\sqrt{LC}$

Before embarking on a study of electron tube oscillators, let us first investigate just what we mean by <u>oscillation</u>. If we take a 100-volt battery and place it across the plates of capacitor C, that capacitor would charge to a value of 100 volts. The actual energy would be in the form of the electrical lines of force existing in the dielectric between the negative and positive plates. On the assumption that C is of perfect quality, the charge would remain forever if the battery were removed. We now place inductor L across C. Since L represents a d-c path for the electrons, C begins to discharge through the inductor. The electron flow through L produces a magnetic field. Thus, in effect, the energy contained in the electric field of C is now transferred into the form of a magnetic field about L. When this magnetic field collapses, electrons flow into C until it is fully charged in the opposite direction, and energy is once more in the form of electric lines of force. When discharging, the reverse occurs and one complete cycle has taken place.

The back-and-forth flow of electrons between C and L is called oscillation. If there were no losses in L and C, these oscillations would continue forever since all the energy stored in the electric and magnetic fields is returned to the circuit. However, due to <u>resistance</u> losses, the energy in each alternation is successively lower. In actual practice, a train of "damped" oscillations occurs, until all the energy is consumed in the form of losses. In the electron tube oscillator, we make use of the L-C circuit characteristics; however, we provide enough <u>additional</u> energy to the circuit on each cycle to make up for the losses during that cycle, giving us continuous oscillations.

Oscillators

An oscillator is a device capable of converting dc into ac at a frequency determined by the values of the constants in the device. Regardless of its type, any oscillator may be divided into three basic elements: the frequency-determining network, the amplifier, and the load or output circuit. From the block diagram, we see the fundamental oscillator components in greater detail. The output power of the amplifier (divided as it is between

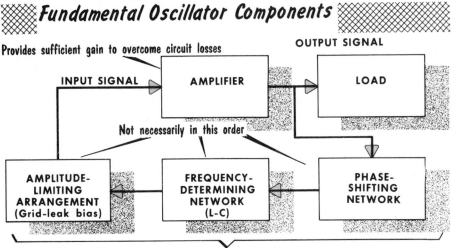

Fundamental Oscillator Components

Provides sufficient gain to overcome circuit losses

OUTPUT SIGNAL

INPUT SIGNAL → AMPLIFIER → LOAD

Not necessarily in this order

AMPLITUDE-LIMITING ARRANGEMENT (Grid-leak bias) ← FREQUENCY-DETERMINING NETWORK (L-C) ← PHASE-SHIFTING NETWORK

FEEDBACK LOOP

the load and the feedback loop) must be sufficiently large to supply both. A second requirement for maintaining oscillation is that the feedback energy and the input energy of the amplifier be in phase. These two specifications can usually be met at only one frequency, since the frequency-determining network changes both the amplitude and phase of its output at frequencies other than the one to which it is tuned.

Starting with the amplifier, the assumption is that some circuit disturbance produces a small voltage change that constitutes input. The amplifier then acts upon this input signal to raise the output power to an adequately high level, so that both the feedback circuit and the load are properly excited. The useful power output remains, of course, in the load. The feedback loop contains the remaining three elements: the phase-shifting network satisfies the requirements of the resonator as far as feedback phase (as related to input phase) is concerned; the frequency-determining network comprises the L-C network, either lumped or distributed, and establishes the oscillator frequency. Finally the amplitude limiting arrangement determines the amount of power to be circulated through the amplifier and feedback loop so that oscillation will neither cease because of insufficient feedback, nor become unstable as a result of excessive feedback. The amplitude-limiting function is usually performed by tube biasing.

Grid-Leak Bias

The generation of oscillations starts with tiny chance disturbances such as non-uniform emission or changes in tube characteristics. The presence of a large Class-C bias at the outset would make it virtually impossible for oscillations to start spontaneously, since the grid signal must exceed the bias voltage. This situation is remedied by starting the cycle of events under conditions of low bias, and building the bias up to Class-C only after the input signal has become large enough. Class-C bias is used for most oscillators because of the high efficiency possible under these conditions. Grid-leak bias provides a natural situation for oscillation. A simple R-C network permits the build-up of oscillation.

In the diagram, the grid of the amplifier is supplied with signal voltage by way of the feedback network. At the beginning of the process, the grid bias is zero with respect to cathode, and the tube operates at a point on its characteristic curve at which the mutual conductance is reasonably high. These conditions encourage easy starting. As the amplitude of the oscillations grows, the alternating voltage appearing across L-C is applied to the grid in series with R_g and C_g. Because of the rectifying action of the grid, dc flows through R_g, causing a voltage having approximately the value of the peak signal voltage to appear across C_g. The development of this bias voltage continues to build up until Class-C operation is established. This is determined by the value of the R-C component in the grid circuit. During the intervals of zero grid current, C_g tends to discharge through R_g. With too short a time constant, no steady-state d-c bias appears, since the capacitor closely follows the variation of the voltage drop across R_g.

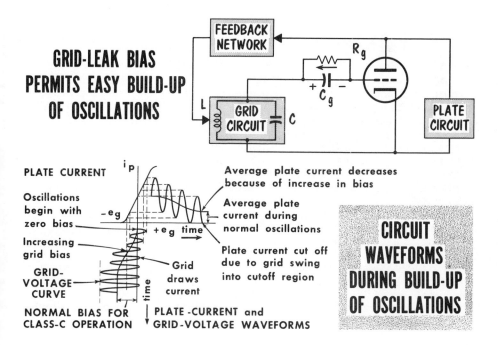

GRID-LEAK BIAS PERMITS EASY BUILD-UP OF OSCILLATIONS

FEEDBACK NETWORK

R_g

C_g

L GRID CIRCUIT   C

PLATE CIRCUIT

PLATE CURRENT

Oscillations begin with zero bias

Increasing grid bias

GRID-VOLTAGE CURVE

NORMAL BIAS FOR CLASS-C OPERATION

i_p

$-e_g$

$+e_g$ time

Average plate current decreases because of increase in bias

Average plate current during normal oscillations

Plate current cut off due to grid swing into cutoff region

Grid draws current

PLATE-CURRENT and GRID-VOLTAGE WAVEFORMS

CIRCUIT WAVEFORMS DURING BUILD-UP OF OSCILLATIONS

The Tickler Feedback (Armstrong) Oscillator

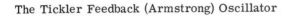

TICKLER-FEEDBACK (ARMSTRONG) OSCILLATOR
can produce a-f and r-f oscillations

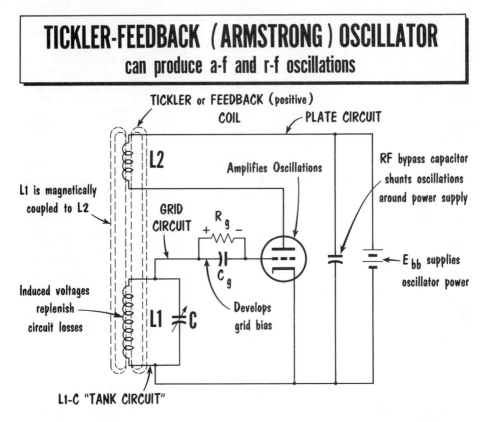

TICKLER or FEEDBACK (positive) COIL

PLATE CIRCUIT

L2

Amplifies Oscillations

RF bypass capacitor shunts oscillations around power supply

L1 is magnetically coupled to L2

GRID CIRCUIT

R_g
+ −

C_g

E_{bb} supplies oscillator power

Induced voltages replenish circuit losses

L1 C

Develops grid bias

L1-C "TANK CIRCUIT"

One of the simplest types of oscillator circuits is that employing tickler feedback. Feedback voltage of the proper phase from the plate circuit to the grid circuit is accomplished by mutual inductive coupling between the oscillator tank coil L1, and the tickler feedback coil, L2. The amount of feedback voltage is determined by the amount of flux from L2 that links L1, and can be varied by moving L2 with respect to L1. The frequency-determining part of the oscillator is the tank circuit L1-C. The coil and tuning capacitor interchange energy at the resonant frequency, and the excitation voltage developed across the tank circuit is applied to the grid in series with the grid-leak bias across R_gC_g.

The tickler coil is coupled to L1 in such a manner that there is regenerative feedback from the plate circuit to the grid circuit. This feedback is sufficient to overcome circuit losses and sustain oscillations in the L1-C circuit. The output or load is generally taken from the oscillating L-C circuit. This has the effect of loading down a circuit. For this reason, the load is considered to increase circuit losses. This can be compensated for by increasing the amount of regenerative feedback. Too great a load damps the oscillations in the L-C circuit, and can cause the oscillations to die out.

The Hartley Oscillator

Along with the Armstrong oscillator, the Hartley oscillator is the most widely used type in radio. L1 is a part of the tuned circuit made up of L1, L2, and C1. It also is used to couple energy from the plate circuit back into the grid circuit by means of mutual inductance between L1 and L2. Cg blocks the d-c component of the grid circuit from L2, and together with Rg provides the necessary operating bias. C2 and the r-f choke keep the a-c component in the plate circuit out of the B supply. The B supply is returned to resonant tank coil L1. The tuned circuit therefore contains a d-c component of plate current in addition to the a-c signal component.

Now let us analyze the operation of this very important oscillator. When the tube warms up, plate current starts to flow, since B+ is applied. Because the grid is located in the electric field between the plate and cathode at a point positive with respect to the cathode, a small positive voltage exists on the grid. The increase in plate current through L1 is accompanied by an expanding magnetic field around L1 which induces voltage e2 in L2. The polarity of e2 makes the grid more positive with respect to the cathode, and plate current continues to increase until saturation. During this time, C1 is charging. Grid current flows as Cg acquires a small charge with the minus side facing the grid. The grid voltage during this time is e2 minus the voltage drop across Cg. Plate current stops increasing at saturation, and the field about L1 stops expanding. As a result, the induced voltage e2 falls to zero. The positive grid voltage (e2 minus the drop across Cg) decreases, causing the plate current to decrease, and C1 begins to discharge.

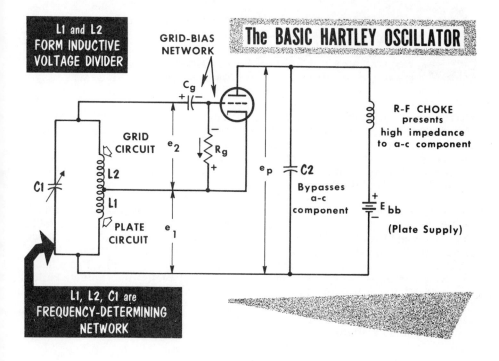

L1 and L2 FORM INDUCTIVE VOLTAGE DIVIDER

GRID-BIAS NETWORK

The BASIC HARTLEY OSCILLATOR

R-F CHOKE presents high impedance to a-c component

GRID CIRCUIT

C_g

e_2

R_g

e_p

$C2$ Bypasses a-c component

E_{bb}

(Plate Supply)

$C1$

L2

L1

PLATE CIRCUIT

e_1

L1, L2, C1 are FREQUENCY-DETERMINING NETWORK

The Hartley Oscillator (Cont'd)

As the field about L1 collapses, it induces voltage e2 in L2 of opposite polarity to e2 when the field was expanding. Hence, the grid voltage goes negative with respect to the cathode, and plate current decreases further. The induced voltage e2 aids in the discharge of C1 and C_g. C1 discharges fully and begins to charge oppositely (its polarity reverses). However, C_g cannot dis-

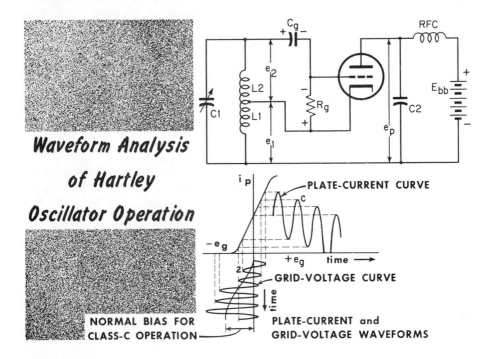

Waveform Analysis of Hartley Oscillator Operation

NORMAL BIAS FOR CLASS-C OPERATION

PLATE-CURRENT and GRID-VOLTAGE WAVEFORMS

charge rapidly because of the long time constant $R_g C_g$. Grid voltage swings to a maximum negative condition (point 2 on grid curve), and C_g discharges slowly through R_g. Grid current does not flow during this part of the cycle, and the grid bias voltage is e2 plus the voltage drop across C_g. Plate current ceases to fall at this point. The field about L1 stops changing and e2 falls to zero. C1 begins to discharge.

The grid bias voltage swings in a positive direction again and plate current begins to rise. The expanding field about L1 again induces voltage e2 in L2, making the grid voltage more positive with respect to cathode. Current flows from cathode to grid into C_g, causing C_g to acquire a small additional charge, while plate current rises to maximum (point C on plate curve). From here, the cycle continues to repeat. On each subsequent cycle, bias voltage builds up across $C_g R_g$ until it reaches a steady value. Normal bias indicates Class-C operation. The flywheel effect of the resonant-tank circuit maintains oscillations during the time that the plate current is zero and no energy is being supplied to the oscillator circuit.

Series and Shunt Feeding

There are two methods for applying plate voltage to the oscillator tube. The d-c plate voltage supply can be placed in series with the oscillating plate circuit, in which case the circuit is referred to as series-fed, or in parallel with the circuit, and the circuit is then referred to as shunt-fed. In either case, there must be a d-c return path from plate to cathode for the plate current. In the series-fed oscillator, the d-c plate current must pass through L1 before it can return to cathode. The disadvantage of this arrangement is that the plate supply is placed at a high a-c potential with respect to the cathode. Also, the supply has a large distributed capacitance to ground that is shunted across tank inductor L1.

The disadvantage of the series-fed circuit can be overcome by keeping the d-c plate supply and the oscillating plate current separate. This is accomplished in the shunt-fed Hartley oscillator where the plate oscillations are

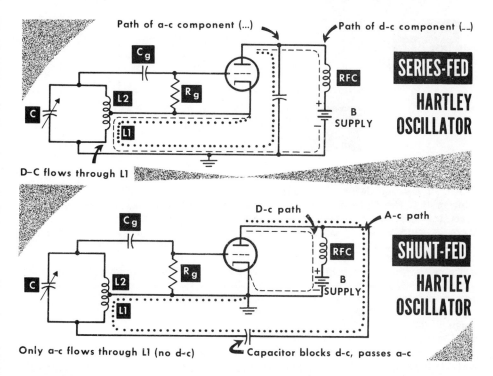

coupled to the split-inductance tank through a bypass capacitor. The capacitor prevents the d-c plate current from returning to the cathode through the tank. The plate current, therefore, can return only through the choke in series with the supply. This choke prevents any oscillations in the supply because its reactance is very high at the oscillation frequency. Thus, the principal advantage of shunt feed is that the high-voltage B supply is isolated from the tuned circuit.

The Colpitts Oscillator

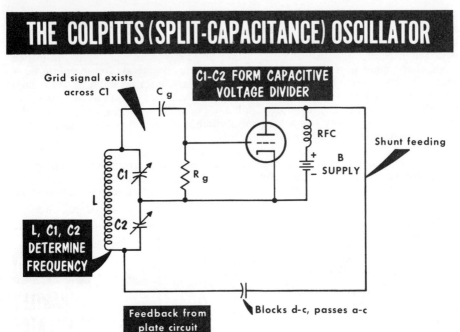

THE COLPITTS (SPLIT-CAPACITANCE) OSCILLATOR

The Colpitts oscillator is similar to the shunt-fed Hartley type, with the exception that the Colpitts uses a split-tank capacitor as part of the feedback circuit instead of a split-tank inductor.   Colpitts oscillators operate extremely well at high frequencies, and stable operation at several hundred megahertz is common.   It is a relatively flexible oscillator because various circuit configurations are possible. Also, it may be made reasonably free of harmonics, and is easy to adjust. The frequency-determining network consists of L, C1, and C2, all connected in series. The plate-circuit signal-return path includes two parallel branches, one through C2 directly to the cathode, and the other through the series combination of L and C1. In this connection, the two tuning capacitors behave as a capacitor voltage divider, and the amount of plate-to-grid feedback depends upon the ratio of C1 to C2. To establish a particular frequency with a given inductance L, capacitors C1 and C2 together must total a specific capacitance; however, the smaller C1 is made and/or the larger C2 becomes, the greater the voltage coupled back will be.   For this reason, both C1 and C2 are usually variable, enabling the operator to establish both the frequency and the amount of feedback.

When R_g is large enough (depending upon the bias required), it does not have much shunt effect upon the signal voltage applied on the grid.   In certain frequencies, at which R_g must be small, an additional choke is necessary, and is inserted in series with R_g.

High-Frequency Oscillators

At very high frequencies, capacitances which are usually ignored, such as interelectrode and stray types, play an extremely important role. At audio and broadcast frequencies, the operating frequency is generally determined by the "lumped" constants of L and C in the circuit. We show a typical high-frequency oscillator often called the ultraudion. There would seem to be no proper feedback arrangement in the basic circuit. However, if d-c bias and plate supply voltages are ignored, and we observe the circuit directly from its a-c "equivalent," we see an arrangement similar to the Colpitts oscillator. The ratio of grid-cathode to plate-cathode alternating voltages is equal to $(C_{pk} + C2)/(C_{gk} + C1)$. The voltage drop across C_{gk} is appreciable at the operating frequency, and provides the grid excitation. The total tank circuit capacitance is equal to the sum of all the "branch" capacitances.

Thus it is obvious that care must be employed in working with high-frequency oscillators, inasmuch as moving wires can change stray capacitances and the substitution of one tube for another can change interelectrode capacitances.

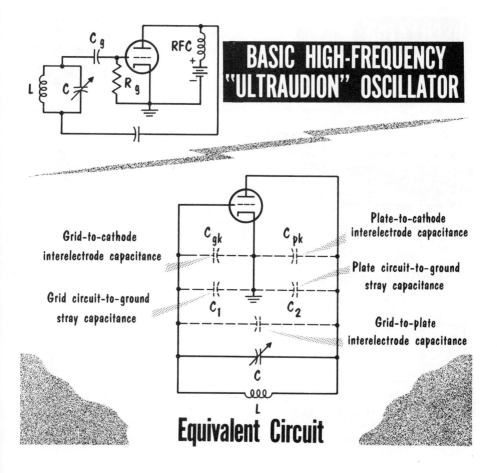

BASIC HIGH-FREQUENCY "ULTRAUDION" OSCILLATOR

Grid-to-cathode interelectrode capacitance

Grid circuit-to-ground stray capacitance

Plate-to-cathode interelectrode capacitance

Plate circuit-to-ground stray capacitance

Grid-to-plate interelectrode capacitance

Equivalent Circuit

The Electron-Coupled Oscillator

As its name implies, the electron-coupled oscillator represents more a form
of coupling than a basically new oscillator circuit. When a load is coupled to
an oscillator tank circuit, the oscillator is subject to frequency variation with
changes in the load. Any changes in the load cause changes in the oscillator
circuit, and consequently a feedback phase shift that tends to make the frequency "drift." Electron coupling is used to isolate the frequency-determining
tank circuit from possible variations due to loading. The use of a pentode
tube, with the screen grid acting as a triode oscillator plate, keeps the plate
circuit independent of the basic oscillator. The oscillations present at the
control grid vary the electron stream flowing from cathode to plate. The
screen grid, however, acts as the primary attracting force for the electrons.
Because of the construction of the screen grid, the major portion of the electron stream goes past the screen and is attracted to the pentode plate where a
voltage is developed across a tuned L-C circuit. The basic circuit used here
is the Hartley; however, any of the oscillators discussed can be used with
electron coupling.

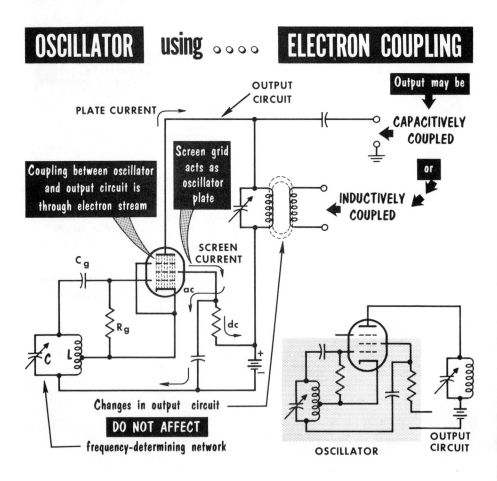

High Frequency Oscillators (UHF and Microwave)

It was noted in the discussion of oscillation in an L-C circuit that the frequency of one cycle of oscillation is determined by the value of L and C and that the frequency is determined by using the formula $2\pi\sqrt{LC}$. To find the value of frequency in hertz we use the formula $f = \dfrac{1}{2\pi\sqrt{LC}}$. From this formula, you can see that <u>increasing</u> the values of inductance and/or capacitance will <u>decrease</u> the resonant frequency of the L-C circuit; conversely, <u>decreasing</u> the values of inductance and/or capacitance will increase the resonant frequency.

In high frequency oscillators, the value of L can be decreased to a point where essentially the only inductances are those of the wire leads leading to the tube socket and those of the wire leads inside the tube. Similarly, the only capacitances are those between the various tube electrodes (which are called interelectrode capacities), the stray capacity between the wire leads, and the capacity between the wire leads and the metal chassis.

During tube operation it takes a specific amount of time for the electrons to leave the cathode and travel to the anode of the tube; this time is referred to as <u>transit time</u>. At low frequencies transit time is of no consequence since it is a very small part of the time required to complete one cycle of oscillation. At high frequencies transit time is important, for example, at 5 gigahertz (5,000 megahertz) each cycle takes one five-billionth of a second to complete. (This is a typical frequency used in satellite communications, radar, etc.) Operating at these frequencies with a conventional tube we would find that when an electron approaches the controlling area of the grid it may find a positive field attracting the electron. By the time the electron reaches the grid the field may have switched to negative, repelling the electron, thus affecting the electron flow within the tube.

The problems of transit time, interelectrode capacities, and stray capacities were originally overcome by the use of special circuits such as the ultraudion oscillator. In time, specially constructed tubes such as the Lighthouse tube, Planar tube, Magnetron, Klystron, and others, were developed. These tubes and circuits are described on the following pages.

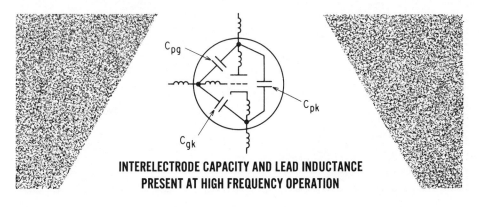

**INTERELECTRODE CAPACITY AND LEAD INDUCTANCE
PRESENT AT HIGH FREQUENCY OPERATION**

Lighthouse (Planar) Oscillator

Construction of a triode with its elements in a flat plane provides a tube useful for operation at frequencies in the range of 2 to 4 GHz. The lighthouse
tube (named because of its resemblance to a lighthouse) shown below has a
flat cathode located directly above the heater filament. The cathode is directly connected to the base pins and capacitively coupled via an insulating
layer to the metal ring above the base. The lead to the base pin is referred
to as the d-c cathode connection and the metal ring is referred to as the r-f
cathode connection. The grid is also constructed on a flat plane and located
close to the cathode. The grid connection is by the smaller circular ring
above the cathode ring. The anode is a cylinder with its flat end above the
grid and connection is made to the anode by a smaller ring and cap. The
planar triode shown below is a newer version of the lighthouse tube, but construction and operation is similar. The major difference in construction is
that the heater is cemented (bonded) directly to the bottom of the cathode surface to provide a mechanically stronger heater.

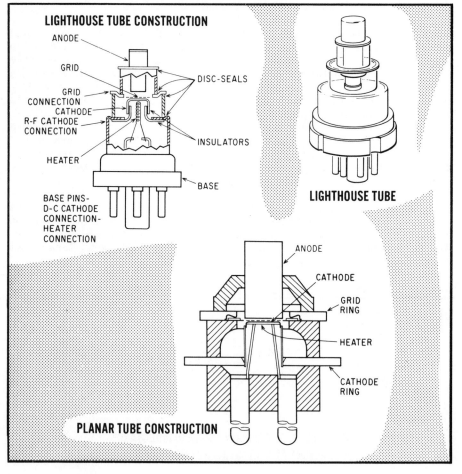

Lighthouse (Planar) Oscillator (Cont'd)

To use the lighthouse tube as a high frequency oscillator the tube has mounted on it three concentric (coaxial) metal cylinders. The cylinders are essentially circular wire leads that provide very low inductive reactance because of their large surface area. The large cylindrical surface area also provides virtually no-loss connections to the anode, grid, and cathode connecting rings. A circular ring of metal between the grid and cathode shorts the two cylinders (there is no d-c path between the grid and r-f cathode). The length of cylinder between the connecting end at the tube and the shorting ring determines the inductance value between the grid and the cathode (L_k) and the capacitance between the grid and cathode (C_{g-k}), shown in the equivalent circuit. The tuning stub for the anode cylinder determines the value of L_p and the capacity between the anode and grid cylinders (C_{g-p}).

The equivalent circuit, a result of the mechanical construction as well as the electrical design, is similar both as a circuit and in operation to the ultraudion and the Colpitts oscillators. An additional difference in the lighthouse oscillator (and in most other high frequency oscillators) is a higher value of anode voltage. The high value of anode voltage accelerates the electron stream flowing from cathode to anode, thereby reducing transit time.

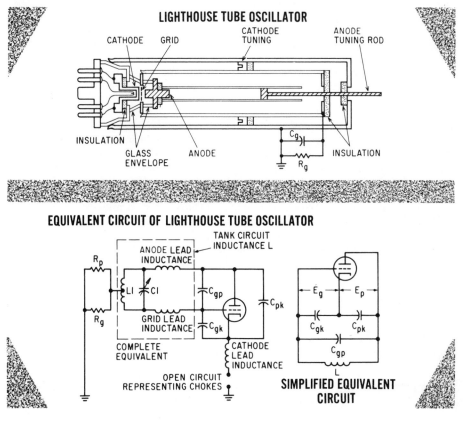

LIGHTHOUSE TUBE OSCILLATOR

EQUIVALENT CIRCUIT OF LIGHTHOUSE TUBE OSCILLATOR

SIMPLIFIED EQUIVALENT CIRCUIT

Magnetron Tube Construction

A tube used to generate frequencies in the range of from 200 MHz to 20 GHz
is the magnetron, so named because it requires a permanent magnet for its
operation. As shown below, the tube has only two main elements, a cathode
and an anode; thus, it is a diode. The heart of the magnetron is the series
of cylindrical holes, called cavities, cut in the copper anode block. Each
cavity can be considered as an L-C tank circuit in which the metal sides represent the inductance, and the capacity between the sides forms the capacitance. The larger the cavity, the larger the values of L-C and, therefore,
the lower the resonant frequency of the cavity. Each cavity represents a
separate L-C oscillatory circuit, with the magnetron using even numbers of
cavities, i.e., 2, 4, 6, etc. By wiring each alternate segment between cavities together with straps, the output of each resonant cavity oscillator is
paralleled. The output is taken from a wire loop placed in one of the cavities
and brought out of the anode block.

The anode-cathode unit is mounted between the poles of a very strong permanent magnet. The method of mounting is such that the lines of force of the
magnetic field flow through all the cavities in the direction of the length of the
cavity.

Carefully centered in the anode block is the circular cathode, which is indirectly heated by an internal filament and held in place by the heavy heater
leads. The space between the cathode and anode is called the "interaction"
space because it is here that the combined magnetic and electric fields inter-
act upon the electrons to cause sustained oscillation. The action of the fields
in the interaction space may be likened to the action of a grid in a conventional triode tube.

The high voltage used in magnetron operation (thousands of volts) and the high
current (e.g., 50A) place the tube at dangerous potentials. To reduce this
problem, the anode is placed at ground (zero) potential and the cathode is
supplied with the high value negative voltage, making the easily accessible
anode block safer. The combination high voltage and high current utilized by
the tube creates a high volume of heat, which may be dissipated by air blow-
ers. For larger magnetron tubes, such as those used in high-power radars,
special demineralized water (or special oil) is cooled and pumped through
and around the tube through special water jackets.

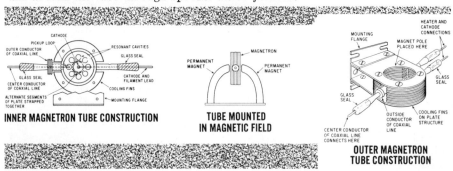

INNER MAGNETRON TUBE CONSTRUCTION

**TUBE MOUNTED
IN MAGNETIC FIELD**

**OUTER MAGNETRON
TUBE CONSTRUCTION**

Magnetron Tube Operation

Although it is harmful to the magnetron to be operated without the magnet, for purposes of discussion we will first assume that only the d-c voltage has been applied. With only the d-c voltage, the electrons will radiate from the cathode in all directions and travel directly to the anode, as shown in A. With application of a weak magnetic field the interaction of the magnetic and electric fields will cause the electrons to be pulled to one side on their way to the anode, as shown in B. Applying a strong magnetic field (C) will cause the electrons to approach, but not reach, the anode (similar to cutoff), and they will loop around and return to the cathode. Application of a very strong magnetic field, however, will cause the electrons that enter the interaction space to be repelled back to the cathode, and at the highly negative cathode the electron is repelled again to move back out to the interaction space, where the process is repeated so that the electrons loop around the cathode in several steps, as shown in D.

During operation, at the application of the high voltage, sufficient electrons reach each cavity to start oscillations. The electrostatic field of electrons revolving about the cathode induces sufficient energy in each cavity to sustain oscillations. The oscillations of each cavity are 180° out of phase with each cavity alongside, thus every other cavity is in phase. This permits the strapping of every other cavity of the even number of cavities to parallel the oscillatory power being generated. As the electrons revolve around the interaction space, the speed of the electrons (determined by the strength of the magnetic field and the strength of the d-c voltage) and the frequency of the oscillations are designed to coincide.

With the correct strength magnetic field and d-c voltage applied, as an electron leaves and circles the cathode it finds an opposing electrostatic field at the first cavity it encounters. This opposition causes the electrons to slow up, and in doing so, the electron loses some energy to the cavity field. This energy, multiplied by the number of electrons involved, is what maintains the high powered oscillations in the cavities. The electron, with reduced energy, is then attracted to the anode, and as it travels to the anode the electron picks up speed, regaining its energy. When the electron approaches the next cavity it repeats the previous action, losing energy to the cavity. This process is repeated a number of times as the electron revolves in the interaction space until finally the electron is pulled close enough to be attracted to the anode.

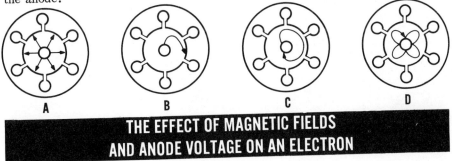

A   B   C   D

THE EFFECT OF MAGNETIC FIELDS
AND ANODE VOLTAGE ON AN ELECTRON

Klystron Oscillators

The klystron is a form of self-oscillating tube originally designed for use in radar receivers. However, newer versions are capable of generating high power for use in transmitters. The basic klystron, shown in A, has the electrons that leave the cathode set up oscillation in both L-C resonant circuits. The oscillations in the first resonant circuit set up an a-c voltage across grids G_1 and G_2. When G_2 is negative and G_1 positive, electrons are repelled by G_2 and accelerated by G_1 causing them to bunch between the grids, thus the name buncher grids. When the cycle is reversed and G_1 is negative, G_1 repels the electrons, keeping them from the buncher grids, reinforcing the buncher action. As the bunches of electrons flow past grids G_3 and G_4 they are timed to impart energy at the proper frequency to sustain the oscillations of the cavity. The action of G_3 and G_4 in "catching" the energy of the bunched electrons gives them the name of catcher grids.

By using the same resonant circuit, in the form of a cavity, as both the buncher and catcher, and by having the electron stream double back (reflex), we have a reflex klystron, shown in B. The control grid, with a fixed positive bias voltage, accelerates the electrons. Varying the control grid varies the density of the electron flow, affecting the output level. The cavity grids, with high values of positive voltage, attract the electrons. (As with the magnetron, the B++ voltage is at ground potential for safety's sake.) The repeller plate, with a high negative voltage, repels the electrons, and has them return and bunch at the cavity grid section. The space between the cavity grids is small, and the action of both grids is cumulative. As the cavity grids swing positive the electron stream is accelerated, and as the grids swing negative the electron stream is repelled. This action, combined with the proper value of repeller voltage, will have some electrons repelled sooner and others repelled later. The combined action has the returned (repelled) electrons bunch at the cavity grids at the right frequency to sustain the oscillations by having the bunched electrons imparting energy to the cavity oscillating circuit.

Changing the repeller voltage can vary the output frequency by a slight amount, thus providing a method for fine tuning. Another method of varying the frequency is by a bellows arrangement of the cavity which permits physically varying the cavity dimensions to vary the output frequency.

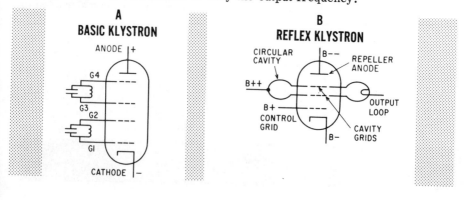

A
BASIC KLYSTRON

B
REFLEX KLYSTRON

Modulation

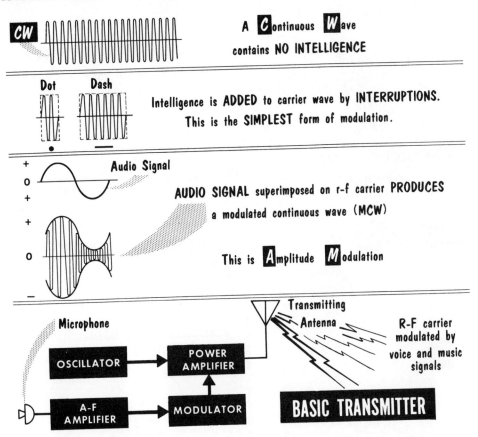

MODULATION is the PROCESS by which INTELLIGENCE is SUPERIMPOSED on a CARRIER WAVE

A **C**ontinuous **W**ave
contains NO INTELLIGENCE

Dot   Dash

Intelligence is ADDED to carrier wave by INTERRUPTIONS.
This is the SIMPLEST form of modulation.

Audio Signal

AUDIO SIGNAL superimposed on r-f carrier PRODUCES
a modulated continuous wave (MCW)

This is **A**mplitude **M**odulation

Microphone

Transmitting
Antenna

R-F carrier
modulated by
voice and music
signals

OSCILLATOR → POWER AMPLIFIER

A-F AMPLIFIER → MODULATOR

BASIC TRANSMITTER

Radio signals are emitted from the transmitting antenna of a radio broadcast station. Basically, the broadcast station generates a powerful train of oscillations called a carrier wave. A circuit in the transmitter called the modulator causes the amplitude of this carrier wave to vary in accordance with the audio intelligence being broadcast. The process of making the amplitude of the carrier wave vary, is known as amplitude modulation (AM). Simple intelligence can be produced merely by a make-and-break process of the carrier wave to form dots and dashes; no real modulator is needed. The modulator is basically nothing more than a powerful audio amplifier. The carrier wave gets its name from actually "carrying" the audio modulation; it serves no other purpose than that. Modulation will be discussed in greater detail in Volume 6.

Demodulation

When the transmitted signal is intercepted by the receiving antenna of the radio receiver, its waveform is identical to that transmitted. It contains the high-frequency r-f carrier component and the audio component in the form of varying amplitude. It is the function of the demodulator circuit in a receiver to

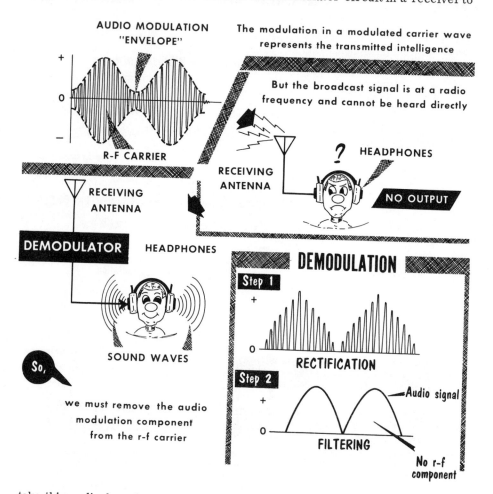

take this radio broadcast signal into its input and produce an audio signal at its output.

The demodulator performs, basically, two tasks: one of rectification, in which the positive or negative alternations of the carrier are removed, and the second of filtering in which the r-f fluctuations are removed leaving only the a-f component or "modulation envelope." In the demodulator, the audio component is still not yet an a-c signal. It is a d-c signal that varies in amplitude at the audio rate.

The Diode Detector

The simplest and most commonly used demodulator is the diode "detector" circuit. Its function is to convert the modulated r-f carrier to a direct current, varying at the a-f rate of the original modulated signal. The diode (tube or crystal) represents an ideal circuit device for signal rectification in that it permits current flow in one direction and not in the other. Because the diode characteristic is nearly straight, the diode detector is called a <u>linear detector</u>. However, with weak signals, the output of the detector follows the "square law," because weak signals force the operation to take place on the lower curved portion of the characteristic. In square-law detection, the output is proportional to the square of the input voltage. Detectors are generally rated in terms of their <u>sensitivity</u> — the ratio of the output signal to the

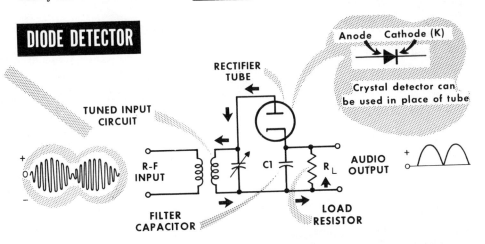

DIODE DETECTOR

Anode Cathode (K)

Crystal detector can be used in place of tube

RECTIFIER TUBE

TUNED INPUT CIRCUIT

R-F INPUT

C1

R_L

AUDIO OUTPUT

FILTER CAPACITOR

LOAD RESISTOR

input signal voltage; <u>linearity</u> — the ability to detect signals throughout the a-f range without distortion; and <u>signal-handling capacity</u> — the ease with which a detector circuit handles a signal without distortion.

The diode detector input is generally a tuned circuit. The other basic components are the diode load resistor and the filter capacitor. The diode detector can handle large signals without overloading, and it can provide an important avc voltage (discussed later) without extra tubes or special circuits. However, it has the disadvantage of drawing power from the input tuned circuit, because the diode and its load form a low-impedance shunt across the circuit. As a result, the circuit Q, the sensitivity, and the selectivity, are reduced. Because the diode detector distorts on weak signals, for optimum operation considerable amplification is needed before detection.

Let us now analyze the action of the diode detector. The incoming modulated r-f signal voltage is developed across the tuned circuit of the detector. Signal current flows through the diode only when the plate is positive with respect to the cathode (only on the positive half-cycles). The rectified signal flowing through the diode actually consists of a series of <u>r-f pulses</u>, and not a smooth outline or "envelope."

Action of the Diode Detector

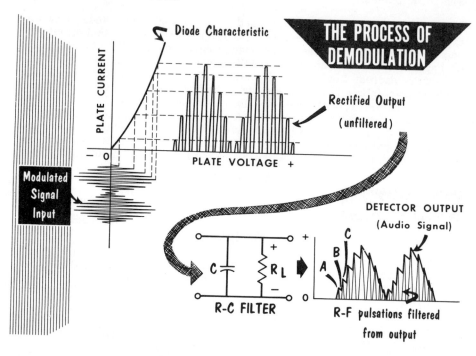

On the first quarter-cycle of the applied r-f voltage, C1 charges almost up to peak value of the r-f voltage (point A). The small voltage drop in the tube prevents C1 from charging up completely. Then, as the applied r-f voltage falls below its applied value, some of the charge of C1 leaks through R_L, and the voltage drops only a small amount to B. When the r-f voltage applied to the plate on the next cycle exceeds the potential at which the capacitor holds the cathode (point B), diode current again flows, and the capacitor charges up to almost the peak value of the second positive cycle at C. Thus, the voltage across C closely follows the peak value of the applied r-f voltage, and reproduces the a-f modulation. The detector output after rectification and filtering is a d-c voltage that varies at an audio rate. The output voltage across C is shown somewhat jagged. Actually, the r-f component of this voltage is negligible, and after amplification, the speech or music originating at the transmitter is faithfully reproduced.

The choice of R_L and C1 in a diode detector is very important for maximum sensitivity and fidelity. R_L and the diode plate resistance act as a voltage divider to the received signal. Therefore, R_L should be high compared with the diode plate resistance for maximum output voltage. In addition, the value of C1 should be such that the R-C time constant is long, compared to the time of one r-f cycle. This is necessary because C must maintain a voltage across R_L during the time there is no plate current. Also, the R-C time constant must be short, compared with the time of one a-f cycle, so that the capacitor voltage can follow the modulation envelope.

The Grid-Leak Detector

The operation of the grid-leak detector is similar to that of the diode detector. The signal voltage applied to the grid of a triode is alternately positive and negative. Grid current flows during the half-cycle in which the grid is positive with respect to the cathode. As a result, pulsating dc flows through R_g. Filter C_g smooths the r-f pulses. A d-c voltage is produced across R_g which varies at an audio rate, just as in the diode detector. This audio voltage is used as the signal voltage input for the triode amplifier. As a result, an amplified audio signal appears in the plate circuit of the grid-leak detector. Capacitor C is an additional r-f filter.

The grid-leak detector is a square-law device, with the output varying as the square of the r-f input voltage. The development of higher-gain r-f amplifiers led to the replacement of the grid-leak detector by the diode detector. In comparison to the diode detector, the grid-leak detector has higher sensitivity, because of its amplification ability, and poorer linearity, because of its operation as a square-law detector. Selectivity is equally poor because it draws grid current through the tank circuit, lowering the Q, and it has a much lower signal-handling ability. The principal advantage of the grid-leak detector is that it provides a stage of audio amplification. The voltage applied to this circuit must not be so high that it causes the average grid voltage to exceed the plate current cutoff voltage for the tube. It is this characteristic that limits the power-handling capacity of the grid-leak detector.

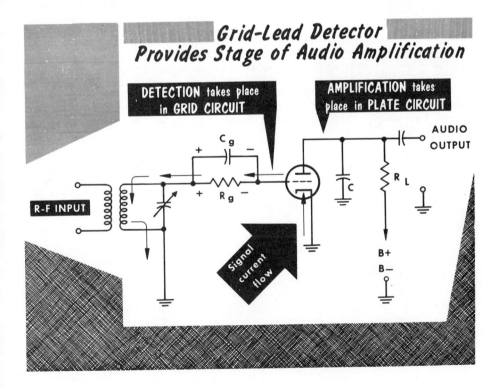

Grid-Lead Detector Provides Stage of Audio Amplification

DETECTION takes place in GRID CIRCUIT

AMPLIFICATION takes place in PLATE CIRCUIT

AUDIO OUTPUT

C_g

R_g

R-F INPUT

C

R_L

Signal current flow

B+
B−

Plate Detector and Infinite Impedance Detector

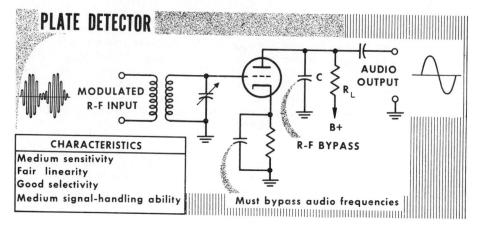

PLATE DETECTOR

MODULATED R-F INPUT

AUDIO OUTPUT

C

R_L

B+

R-F BYPASS

CHARACTERISTICS
Medium sensitivity
Fair linearity
Good selectivity
Medium signal-handling ability

Must bypass audio frequencies

The <u>plate detector</u> gets its name because detection occurs in the plate circuit. Operation is similar to that of a Class-B amplifier. Although cathode bias cannot produce plate current cutoff, operation at the lower end of the dynamic characteristic is possible. Normal plate current flows during the positive half-cycle of the input signal, with most of the negative half-cycle cut off. As a result, the average value of the plate current varies in accordance with the audio variations. Capacitor C acts as an r-f filter.

If the plate of the plate detector is connected directly to B+ and the output is taken across the cathode network, the result is an <u>infinite impedance detector</u>. Although there is no amplification of the signal in this circuit, which has the advantage of good reproduction, it has good signal-handling capacity for large inputs. The modulated r-f signal varies the d-c plate current through the tube. This current returning to the cathode network is filtered through C_k, and the current passing through R_k is dc, varying at an audio rate with negligible r-f ripple.

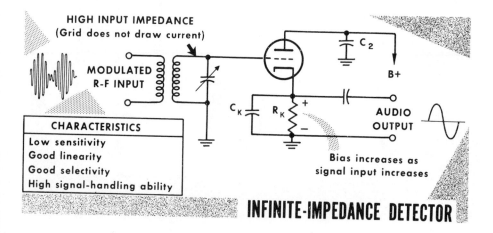

HIGH INPUT IMPEDANCE
(Grid does not draw current)

MODULATED R-F INPUT

C_2

B+

C_K R_K +   −

AUDIO OUTPUT

CHARACTERISTICS
Low sensitivity
Good linearity
Good selectivity
High signal-handling ability

Bias increases as signal input increases

INFINITE-IMPEDANCE DETECTOR

To produce oscillations, an electron tube circuit must contain a tuned circuit having the proper amounts of inductance and capacitance to oscillate at the desired frequency; it must be capable of amplifying a signal at its control grid; it must have a means of providing the tuned circuit with sufficient regenerative energy to sustain oscillations.

The tuned grid oscillator obtains regenerative or positive feedback by coupling the plate circuit to the tuned grid circuit.

There are two basic types of split-tank oscillators — the Hartley and the Colpitts. The Hartley oscillator has a split-inductance tank divided between the grid and plate circuits; the Colpitts oscillator has a split-capacitance tank divided between the grid and plate circuits.

An oscillator is shunt-fed when its d-c plate supply is in parallel with the oscillating plate circuit.

The electron-coupled oscillator replaces the separate oscillator with an oscillator having "insulation" from loading effects. Coupling to the output circuit is through the electron stream in the tube.

Bias for r-f amplifiers is usually obtained from the action of the grid drawing current during part of the input cycle.

Oscillators generally use grid-leak bias.

Ultra high frequencies (microwaves) are developed by using specially constructed tubes with very low interelectrode capacities.

Demodulation is the process by which a circuit separates the modulation component from the r-f component of a carrier wave.

The simple diode detector is the most commonly used demodulator.

Modulation is the process in which intelligence is superimposed on the r-f carrier wave at the broadcast station.

The grid-leak detector provides a high degree of sensitivity; however, its selectivity is poor.

The signal-handling ability of a detector is an indication of the amount of signal amplitude that can be handled without overloading the circuit. The sharpness with which a detector can be tuned determines its selectivity. The amount of distortion in the a-f signal as compared with the original sound is a measure of the linearity of a detector. A detector providing some amplification has greater sensitivity than one providing no amplification.

REVIEW QUESTIONS

1. Why does a damped oscillation occur in an L-C circuit?
2. Under what conditions can oscillations be maintained in an L-C circuit?
3. What is the function of the amplifier in an electron-tube oscillator?
4. Name the basic types of split-tank oscillators.
5. Explain the operation of the electron-coupled oscillator.
6. Explain how grid-leak bias is developed in an oscillator.
7. Explain the operation of the Armstrong oscillator.
8. Explain transit time.
9. Explain the fundamental characteristics of modulation and demodulation.
10. Explain how detection takes place in the diode detector.
11. Explain the operation of the grid-leak detector.
12. Compare the sensitivity of the diode, grid-leak, and plate detectors.

GLOSSARY

Amplification Factor: The ratio of a small change in plate voltage to a small change in grid voltage, with all other electrode voltages constant, required to produce tthe same change in plate current.

Amplifier: A device used to increase the signal voltage, current, or power, generally composed of a vacuum tube and associated circuit. It may contain several stages to obtain a desired gain.

Anode: A positive electrode. The plate of a vacuum tube.

Audio Frequency: A range of frequencies that can be detected as a sound by the human ear.

Beam-Power Tube: A vacuum tube in which the electron stream is directed in concentrated beams from the cathode to the plate.

Bias: The average d-c voltage maintained between the cathode and control grid of a vacuum tube.

Blocking Capacitor: A capacitor used to block the flow of dc while permitting the flow of ac.

Cathode: Negatively charged pole, electrode, conductor, or element from which current leaves. The primary source of electrons in a vacuum tube.

Coupling: The association of two circuits in such a way that energy may be transferred from one to the other.

Cutoff: The minimum value of negative grid bias which prevents the flow of plate current in a vacuum tube.

Detection: The process of separating the modulation component from the received signal.

Diode: A two-electrode vacuum tube containing a cathode and a plate.

Distortion: The production an an output waveform which is not a true reproduction of the input waveform.

Dynamic Characteristics: The relationship between the instantaneous plate voltage and plate current of a vacuum tube as the voltage applied to the grid is moved; thus, the characteristics of a vacuum tube during operation.

Feedback: A transfer of energy from the output circuit of a device back to its input.

Gain: The ratio of the output power, voltage, or current to the input power, voltage, or current respectively.

Grid: An electrode consisting of a wire mesh placed between cathode and plate in an electron tube, and used to control the electron flow through the tube.

Intermediate Frequency: The fixed frequency to which r-f carrier waves are converted in a superheterodyne receiver.

Local Oscillator: The oscillator used in a superheterodyne receiver, the output of which is mixed with the desired r-f carrier to form the intermediate frequency.

Microwave Oscillator: Oscillator circuit generating ultrahigh frequencies through the use of specially constructed tubes.

Modulation: The process of varying the amplitude (AM), the frequency (FM), or the phase (PM) of a carrier wave in accordance with other signals to convey intelligence.

Negative Feedback: The process whereby a part of the output signal of an amplifying device is returned to the input circuit in such a manner that it tends to cancel the input.

Oscillator: A circuit capable of converting dc into ac of a frequency determined by the constants of the circuit.

Paraphase Amplifier: An amplifier which converts a single input into a push-pull output.

Pentode: A five-electrode vacuum tube containing, a cathode, control grid, screen grid, suppressor grid, and plate.

Plate: The principal electrode in a tube to which the electron stream is attracted.

Plate-Load Impedance: The impedance in the plate circuit across which the output-signal voltage is developed by the alternating component of the plate current.

Plate Resistance: The internal resistance to the flow of ac between the cathode and plate of a tube. It is equal to a small change in plate voltage divided by the corresponding change in plate current, and is expressed in ohms.

Power Amplification: The process of amplifying a signal to produce a gain in power, as distinguished from voltage amplification.

Push-Pull Circuit: An amplifier circuit using two vacuum tubes in such a way that when one tube is operating on a positive alternation, the other operates on a negative alternation.

Radio Frequency: Any frequency of electrical energy capable of propagation into space.

Radio-Frequency Amplification: The amplification of a radio wave by a receiver before detection.

Rectifier: A device that changes alternating current into unidirectional current.

Self Bias: The bias of a tube created by the voltage drop developed across a resistor through which either its cathode or its grid current flows.

Shielding: A metallic covering to prevent magnetic or electrostatic coupling between adjacent circuits.

Space Current: The total current flowing between cathode and all the other electrodes in a tube. This includes the plate current, grid current, screen-grid current, and any other electrode current which may be present.

Static Characteristics: The characteristics of a tube with no output load and with d-c voltages applied to the grid and plate.

Superheterodyne: A receiver in which the incoming signal is mixed with a locally generated signal to produce a predetermined intermediate frequency.

Suppressor Grid: An electrode used in a vacuum tube to minimize the harmful effects of secondary emission from the plate.

Tetrode: A four-electrode vacuum tube containing a cathode, control grid, screen grid, and plate.

Thermionic Emission: Electron emission caused by heating an emitter.

Transconductance: The ratio of the change in plate current to the change in grid voltage producing this change in plate current, while all other electrode voltages remain constant.

Triode: A three-electrode vacuum tube, containing a cathode, control grid, and plate.

Vacuum Tube: Device consisting of an evacuated enclosure containing a number of electrodes that control the conduction of electrons through the vacuum.

Variable-mu tube: A vacuum tube in which the control grid is irregularly spaced, so that the grid exercises a different amount of control on the electron stream at different points within its operating range.

Voltage Regulation: A measure of the degree to which a power source maintains its output voltage stability under varying load conditions.

Voltage Amplification. The process of amplifying a signal to produce a gain in voltage. The voltage gain of an amplifier is the ratio of its alternating voltage output to its alternating voltage input.

INDEX
Vol. 3

(Note: A cumulative index covering all six volumes in this series is included at the end of Volume 6.)